C-897　　CAREER EXAMINATION SERIES

This is your
PASSBOOK for...

Water Plant Operator

Test Preparation Study Guide
Questions & Answers

COPYRIGHT NOTICE

This book is SOLELY intended for, is sold ONLY to, and its use is RESTRICTED to individual, bona fide applicants or candidates who qualify by virtue of having seriously filed applications for appropriate license, certificate, professional and/or promotional advancement, higher school matriculation, scholarship, or other legitimate requirements of education and/or governmental authorities.

This book is NOT intended for use, class instruction, tutoring, training, duplication, copying, reprinting, excerption, or adaptation, etc., by:

1) Other publishers
2) Proprietors and/or Instructors of "Coaching" and/or Preparatory Courses
3) Personnel and/or Training Divisions of commercial, industrial, and governmental organizations
4) Schools, colleges, or universities and/or their departments and staffs, including teachers and other personnel
5) Testing Agencies or Bureaus
6) Study groups which seek by the purchase of a single volume to copy and/or duplicate and/or adapt this material for use by the group as a whole without having purchased individual volumes for each of the members of the group
7) Et al.

Such persons would be in violation of appropriate Federal and State statutes.

PROVISION OF LICENSING AGREEMENTS – Recognized educational, commercial, industrial, and governmental institutions and organizations, and others legitimately engaged in educational pursuits, including training, testing, and measurement activities, may address request for a licensing agreement to the copyright owners, who will determine whether, and under what conditions, including fees and charges, the materials in this book may be used them. In other words, a licensing facility exists for the legitimate use of the material in this book on other than an individual basis. However, it is asseverated and affirmed here that the material in this book CANNOT be used without the receipt of the express permission of such a licensing agreement from the Publishers. Inquiries re licensing should be addressed to the company, attention rights and permissions department.

All rights reserved, including the right of reproduction in whole or in part, in any form or by any means, electronic or mechanical, including photocopying, recording, or by any information storage and retrieval system, without permission in writing from the Publisher.

Copyright © 2025 by
National Learning Corporation

212 Michael Drive, Syosset, NY 11791
(516) 921-8888 • www.passbooks.com
E-mail: info@passbooks.com

PASSBOOK® SERIES

THE *PASSBOOK® SERIES* has been created to prepare applicants and candidates for the ultimate academic battlefield – the examination room.

At some time in our lives, each and every one of us may be required to take an examination – for validation, matriculation, admission, qualification, registration, certification, or licensure.

Based on the assumption that every applicant or candidate has met the basic formal educational standards, has taken the required number of courses, and read the necessary texts, the *PASSBOOK® SERIES* furnishes the one special preparation which may assure passing with confidence, instead of failing with insecurity. Examination questions – together with answers – are furnished as the basic vehicle for study so that the mysteries of the examination and its compounding difficulties may be eliminated or diminished by a sure method.

This book is meant to help you pass your examination provided that you qualify and are serious in your objective.

The entire field is reviewed through the huge store of content information which is succinctly presented through a provocative and challenging approach – the question-and-answer method.

A climate of success is established by furnishing the correct answers at the end of each test.

You soon learn to recognize types of questions, forms of questions, and patterns of questioning. You may even begin to anticipate expected outcomes.

You perceive that many questions are repeated or adapted so that you can gain acute insights, which may enable you to score many sure points.

You learn how to confront new questions, or types of questions, and to attack them confidently and work out the correct answers.

You note objectives and emphases, and recognize pitfalls and dangers, so that you may make positive educational adjustments.

Moreover, you are kept fully informed in relation to new concepts, methods, practices, and directions in the field.

You discover that you are actually taking the examination all the time: you are preparing for the examination by "taking" an examination, not by reading extraneous and/or supererogatory textbooks.

In short, this PASSBOOK®, used directedly, should be an important factor in helping you to pass your test.

WATER PLANT OPERATOR

DUTIES
Under supervision, operates and maintains machinery and equipment of a water plant and allied pumping stations in a water purification and distribution system. Does related work as required.

SUBJECT OF EXAMINATION
Written test designed to test for knowledge, skills and/or abilities in such areas as:
1. Practices and equipment used in the operation and maintenance of a water treatment plant;
2. Principles and application of chemistry and general science as related to water treatment and purification;
3. Operation, maintenance, and repair of pumps, motors, valves, electrical and mechanical equipment;
4. Tools, mechanical aptitude, and the reading of scales and gauges;
5. Understanding and interpreting written material; and
6. Basic mathematics.

HOW TO TAKE A TEST

I. YOU MUST PASS AN EXAMINATION

A. WHAT EVERY CANDIDATE SHOULD KNOW

Examination applicants often ask us for help in preparing for the written test. What can I study in advance? What kinds of questions will be asked? How will the test be given? How will the papers be graded?

As an applicant for a civil service examination, you may be wondering about some of these things. Our purpose here is to suggest effective methods of advance study and to describe civil service examinations.

Your chances for success on this examination can be increased if you know how to prepare. Those "pre-examination jitters" can be reduced if you know what to expect. You can even experience an adventure in good citizenship if you know why civil service exams are given.

B. WHY ARE CIVIL SERVICE EXAMINATIONS GIVEN?

Civil service examinations are important to you in two ways. As a citizen, you want public jobs filled by employees who know how to do their work. As a job seeker, you want a fair chance to compete for that job on an equal footing with other candidates. The best-known means of accomplishing this two-fold goal is the competitive examination.

Exams are widely publicized throughout the nation. They may be administered for jobs in federal, state, city, municipal, town or village governments or agencies.

Any citizen may apply, with some limitations, such as the age or residence of applicants. Your experience and education may be reviewed to see whether you meet the requirements for the particular examination. When these requirements exist, they are reasonable and applied consistently to all applicants. Thus, a competitive examination may cause you some uneasiness now, but it is your privilege and safeguard.

C. HOW ARE CIVIL SERVICE EXAMS DEVELOPED?

Examinations are carefully written by trained technicians who are specialists in the field known as "psychological measurement," in consultation with recognized authorities in the field of work that the test will cover. These experts recommend the subject matter areas or skills to be tested; only those knowledges or skills important to your success on the job are included. The most reliable books and source materials available are used as references. Together, the experts and technicians judge the difficulty level of the questions.

Test technicians know how to phrase questions so that the problem is clearly stated. Their ethics do not permit "trick" or "catch" questions. Questions may have been tried out on sample groups, or subjected to statistical analysis, to determine their usefulness.

Written tests are often used in combination with performance tests, ratings of training and experience, and oral interviews. All of these measures combine to form the best-known means of finding the right person for the right job.

II. HOW TO PASS THE WRITTEN TEST

A. NATURE OF THE EXAMINATION

To prepare intelligently for civil service examinations, you should know how they differ from school examinations you have taken. In school you were assigned certain definite pages to read or subjects to cover. The examination questions were quite detailed and usually emphasized memory. Civil service exams, on the other hand, try to discover your present ability to perform the duties of a position, plus your potentiality to learn these duties. In other words, a civil service exam attempts to predict how successful you will be. Questions cover such a broad area that they cannot be as minute and detailed as school exam questions.

In the public service similar kinds of work, or positions, are grouped together in one "class." This process is known as *position-classification*. All the positions in a class are paid according to the salary range for that class. One class title covers all of these positions, and they are all tested by the same examination.

B. FOUR BASIC STEPS

1) Study the announcement

How, then, can you know what subjects to study? Our best answer is: "Learn as much as possible about the class of positions for which you've applied." The exam will test the knowledge, skills and abilities needed to do the work.

Your most valuable source of information about the position you want is the official exam announcement. This announcement lists the training and experience qualifications. Check these standards and apply only if you come reasonably close to meeting them.

The brief description of the position in the examination announcement offers some clues to the subjects which will be tested. Think about the job itself. Review the duties in your mind. Can you perform them, or are there some in which you are rusty? Fill in the blank spots in your preparation.

Many jurisdictions preview the written test in the exam announcement by including a section called "Knowledge and Abilities Required," "Scope of the Examination," or some similar heading. Here you will find out specifically what fields will be tested.

2) Review your own background

Once you learn in general what the position is all about, and what you need to know to do the work, ask yourself which subjects you already know fairly well and which need improvement. You may wonder whether to concentrate on improving your strong areas or on building some background in your fields of weakness. When the announcement has specified "some knowledge" or "considerable knowledge," or has used adjectives like "beginning principles of..." or "advanced ... methods," you can get a clue as to the number and difficulty of questions to be asked in any given field. More questions, and hence broader coverage, would be included for those subjects which are more important in the work. Now weigh your strengths and weaknesses against the job requirements and prepare accordingly.

3) Determine the level of the position

Another way to tell how intensively you should prepare is to understand the level of the job for which you are applying. Is it the entering level? In other words, is this the position in which beginners in a field of work are hired? Or is it an intermediate or advanced level? Sometimes this is indicated by such words as "Junior" or "Senior" in the class title. Other jurisdictions use Roman numerals to designate the level – Clerk I, Clerk II, for example. The word "Supervisor" sometimes appears in the title. If the level is not indicated by the title, check the description of duties. Will you be working under very close supervision, or will you have responsibility for independent decisions in this work?

4) Choose appropriate study materials

Now that you know the subjects to be examined and the relative amount of each subject to be covered, you can choose suitable study materials. For beginning level jobs, or even advanced ones, if you have a pronounced weakness in some aspect of your training, read a modern, standard textbook in that field. Be sure it is up to date and has general coverage. Such books are normally available at your library, and the librarian will be glad to help you locate one. For entry-level positions, questions of appropriate difficulty are chosen – neither highly advanced questions, nor those too simple. Such questions require careful thought but not advanced training.

If the position for which you are applying is technical or advanced, you will read more advanced, specialized material. If you are already familiar with the basic principles of your field, elementary textbooks would waste your time. Concentrate on advanced textbooks and technical periodicals. Think through the concepts and review difficult problems in your field.

These are all general sources. You can get more ideas on your own initiative, following these leads. For example, training manuals and publications of the government agency which employs workers in your field can be useful, particularly for technical and professional positions. A letter or visit to the government department involved may result in more specific study suggestions, and certainly will provide you with a more definite idea of the exact nature of the position you are seeking.

III. KINDS OF TESTS

Tests are used for purposes other than measuring knowledge and ability to perform specified duties. For some positions, it is equally important to test ability to make adjustments to new situations or to profit from training. In others, basic mental abilities not dependent on information are essential. Questions which test these things may not appear as pertinent to the duties of the position as those which test for knowledge and information. Yet they are often highly important parts of a fair examination. For very general questions, it is almost impossible to help you direct your study efforts. What we can do is to point out some of the more common of these general abilities needed in public service positions and describe some typical questions.

1) General information

Broad, general information has been found useful for predicting job success in some kinds of work. This is tested in a variety of ways, from vocabulary lists to questions about current events. Basic background in some field of work, such as sociology or economics, may be sampled in a group of questions. Often these are principles which have become familiar to most persons through exposure rather than through formal training. It is difficult to advise you how to study for these questions; being alert to the world around you is our best suggestion.

2) Verbal ability

An example of an ability needed in many positions is verbal or language ability. Verbal ability is, in brief, the ability to use and understand words. Vocabulary and grammar tests are typical measures of this ability. Reading comprehension or paragraph interpretation questions are common in many kinds of civil service tests. You are given a paragraph of written material and asked to find its central meaning.

3) Numerical ability

Number skills can be tested by the familiar arithmetic problem, by checking paired lists of numbers to see which are alike and which are different, or by interpreting charts and graphs. In the latter test, a graph may be printed in the test booklet which you are asked to use as the basis for answering questions.

4) Observation

A popular test for law-enforcement positions is the observation test. A picture is shown to you for several minutes, then taken away. Questions about the picture test your ability to observe both details and larger elements.

5) Following directions

In many positions in the public service, the employee must be able to carry out written instructions dependably and accurately. You may be given a chart with several columns, each column listing a variety of information. The questions require you to carry out directions involving the information given in the chart.

6) Skills and aptitudes

Performance tests effectively measure some manual skills and aptitudes. When the skill is one in which you are trained, such as typing or shorthand, you can practice. These tests are often very much like those given in business school or high school courses. For many of the other skills and aptitudes, however, no short-time preparation can be made. Skills and abilities natural to you or that you have developed throughout your lifetime are being tested.

Many of the general questions just described provide all the data needed to answer the questions and ask you to use your reasoning ability to find the answers. Your best preparation for these tests, as well as for tests of facts and ideas, is to be at your physical and mental best. You, no doubt, have your own methods of getting into an exam-taking mood and keeping "in shape." The next section lists some ideas on this subject.

IV. KINDS OF QUESTIONS

Only rarely is the "essay" question, which you answer in narrative form, used in civil service tests. Civil service tests are usually of the short-answer type. Full instructions for answering these questions will be given to you at the examination. But in case this is your first experience with short-answer questions and separate answer sheets, here is what you need to know:

1) Multiple-choice Questions

Most popular of the short-answer questions is the "multiple choice" or "best answer" question. It can be used, for example, to test for factual knowledge, ability to solve problems or judgment in meeting situations found at work.

A multiple-choice question is normally one of three types—
- It can begin with an incomplete statement followed by several possible endings. You are to find the one ending which *best* completes the statement, although some of the others may not be entirely wrong.
- It can also be a complete statement in the form of a question which is answered by choosing one of the statements listed.

- It can be in the form of a problem – again you select the best answer.

Here is an example of a multiple-choice question with a discussion which should give you some clues as to the method for choosing the right answer:

When an employee has a complaint about his assignment, the action which will *best* help him overcome his difficulty is to
- A. discuss his difficulty with his coworkers
- B. take the problem to the head of the organization
- C. take the problem to the person who gave him the assignment
- D. say nothing to anyone about his complaint

In answering this question, you should study each of the choices to find which is best. Consider choice "A" – Certainly an employee may discuss his complaint with fellow employees, but no change or improvement can result, and the complaint remains unresolved. Choice "B" is a poor choice since the head of the organization probably does not know what assignment you have been given, and taking your problem to him is known as "going over the head" of the supervisor. The supervisor, or person who made the assignment, is the person who can clarify it or correct any injustice. Choice "C" is, therefore, correct. To say nothing, as in choice "D," is unwise. Supervisors have and interest in knowing the problems employees are facing, and the employee is seeking a solution to his problem.

2) True/False Questions

The "true/false" or "right/wrong" form of question is sometimes used. Here a complete statement is given. Your job is to decide whether the statement is right or wrong.

SAMPLE: A roaming cell-phone call to a nearby city costs less than a non-roaming call to a distant city.

This statement is wrong, or false, since roaming calls are more expensive.

This is not a complete list of all possible question forms, although most of the others are variations of these common types. You will always get complete directions for answering questions. Be sure you understand *how* to mark your answers – ask questions until you do.

V. RECORDING YOUR ANSWERS

Computer terminals are used more and more today for many different kinds of exams.

For an examination with very few applicants, you may be told to record your answers in the test booklet itself. Separate answer sheets are much more common. If this separate answer sheet is to be scored by machine – and this is often the case – it is highly important that you mark your answers correctly in order to get credit.

An electronic scoring machine is often used in civil service offices because of the speed with which papers can be scored. Machine-scored answer sheets must be marked with a pencil, which will be given to you. This pencil has a high graphite content which responds to the electronic scoring machine. As a matter of fact, stray dots may register as answers, so do not let your pencil rest on the answer sheet while you are pondering the correct answer. Also, if your pencil lead breaks or is otherwise defective, ask for another.

Since the answer sheet will be dropped in a slot in the scoring machine, be careful not to bend the corners or get the paper crumpled.

The answer sheet normally has five vertical columns of numbers, with 30 numbers to a column. These numbers correspond to the question numbers in your test booklet. After each number, going across the page are four or five pairs of dotted lines. These short dotted lines have small letters or numbers above them. The first two pairs may also have a "T" or "F" above the letters. This indicates that the first two pairs only are to be used if the questions are of the true-false type. If the questions are multiple choice, disregard the "T" and "F" and pay attention only to the small letters or numbers.

Answer your questions in the manner of the sample that follows:

32. The largest city in the United States is
    A. Washington, D.C.
    B. New York City
    C. Chicago
    D. Detroit
    E. San Francisco

1) Choose the answer you think is best. (New York City is the largest, so "B" is correct.)
2) Find the row of dotted lines numbered the same as the question you are answering. (Find row number 32)
3) Find the pair of dotted lines corresponding to the answer. (Find the pair of lines under the mark "B.")
4) Make a solid black mark between the dotted lines.

VI. BEFORE THE TEST

Common sense will help you find procedures to follow to get ready for an examination. Too many of us, however, overlook these sensible measures. Indeed, nervousness and fatigue have been found to be the most serious reasons why applicants fail to do their best on civil service tests. Here is a list of reminders:

- Begin your preparation early – Don't wait until the last minute to go scurrying around for books and materials or to find out what the position is all about.
- Prepare continuously – An hour a night for a week is better than an all-night cram session. This has been definitely established. What is more, a night a week for a month will return better dividends than crowding your study into a shorter period of time.
- Locate the place of the exam – You have been sent a notice telling you when and where to report for the examination. If the location is in a different town or otherwise unfamiliar to you, it would be well to inquire the best route and learn something about the building.
- Relax the night before the test – Allow your mind to rest. Do not study at all that night. Plan some mild recreation or diversion; then go to bed early and get a good night's sleep.
- Get up early enough to make a leisurely trip to the place for the test – This way unforeseen events, traffic snarls, unfamiliar buildings, etc. will not upset you.
- Dress comfortably – A written test is not a fashion show. You will be known by number and not by name, so wear something comfortable.

- Leave excess paraphernalia at home – Shopping bags and odd bundles will get in your way. You need bring only the items mentioned in the official notice you received; usually everything you need is provided. Do not bring reference books to the exam. They will only confuse those last minutes and be taken away from you when in the test room.
- Arrive somewhat ahead of time – If because of transportation schedules you must get there very early, bring a newspaper or magazine to take your mind off yourself while waiting.
- Locate the examination room – When you have found the proper room, you will be directed to the seat or part of the room where you will sit. Sometimes you are given a sheet of instructions to read while you are waiting. Do not fill out any forms until you are told to do so; just read them and be prepared.
- Relax and prepare to listen to the instructions
- If you have any physical problem that may keep you from doing your best, be sure to tell the test administrator. If you are sick or in poor health, you really cannot do your best on the exam. You can come back and take the test some other time.

VII. AT THE TEST

The day of the test is here and you have the test booklet in your hand. The temptation to get going is very strong. Caution! There is more to success than knowing the right answers. You must know how to identify your papers and understand variations in the type of short-answer question used in this particular examination. Follow these suggestions for maximum results from your efforts:

1) Cooperate with the monitor

The test administrator has a duty to create a situation in which you can be as much at ease as possible. He will give instructions, tell you when to begin, check to see that you are marking your answer sheet correctly, and so on. He is not there to guard you, although he will see that your competitors do not take unfair advantage. He wants to help you do your best.

2) Listen to all instructions

Don't jump the gun! Wait until you understand all directions. In most civil service tests you get more time than you need to answer the questions. So don't be in a hurry. Read each word of instructions until you clearly understand the meaning. Study the examples, listen to all announcements and follow directions. Ask questions if you do not understand what to do.

3) Identify your papers

Civil service exams are usually identified by number only. You will be assigned a number; you must not put your name on your test papers. Be sure to copy your number correctly. Since more than one exam may be given, copy your exact examination title.

4) Plan your time

Unless you are told that a test is a "speed" or "rate of work" test, speed itself is usually not important. Time enough to answer all the questions will be provided, but this does not mean that you have all day. An overall time limit has been set. Divide the total time (in minutes) by the number of questions to determine the approximate time you have for each question.

5) Do not linger over difficult questions

If you come across a difficult question, mark it with a paper clip (useful to have along) and come back to it when you have been through the booklet. One caution if you do this – be sure to skip a number on your answer sheet as well. Check often to be sure that you have not lost your place and that you are marking in the row numbered the same as the question you are answering.

6) Read the questions

Be sure you know what the question asks! Many capable people are unsuccessful because they failed to *read* the questions correctly.

7) Answer all questions

Unless you have been instructed that a penalty will be deducted for incorrect answers, it is better to guess than to omit a question.

8) Speed tests

It is often better NOT to guess on speed tests. It has been found that on timed tests people are tempted to spend the last few seconds before time is called in marking answers at random – without even reading them – in the hope of picking up a few extra points. To discourage this practice, the instructions may warn you that your score will be "corrected" for guessing. That is, a penalty will be applied. The incorrect answers will be deducted from the correct ones, or some other penalty formula will be used.

9) Review your answers

If you finish before time is called, go back to the questions you guessed or omitted to give them further thought. Review other answers if you have time.

10) Return your test materials

If you are ready to leave before others have finished or time is called, take ALL your materials to the monitor and leave quietly. Never take any test material with you. The monitor can discover whose papers are not complete, and taking a test booklet may be grounds for disqualification.

VIII. EXAMINATION TECHNIQUES

1) Read the general instructions carefully. These are usually printed on the first page of the exam booklet. As a rule, these instructions refer to the timing of the examination; the fact that you should not start work until the signal and must stop work at a signal, etc. If there are any *special* instructions, such as a choice of questions to be answered, make sure that you note this instruction carefully.

2) When you are ready to start work on the examination, that is as soon as the signal has been given, read the instructions to each question booklet, underline any key words or phrases, such as *least, best, outline, describe* and the like. In this way you will tend to answer as requested rather than discover on reviewing your paper that you *listed without describing*, that you selected the *worst* choice rather than the *best* choice, etc.

3) If the examination is of the objective or multiple-choice type – that is, each question will also give a series of possible answers: A, B, C or D, and you are called upon to select the best answer and write the letter next to that answer on your answer paper – it is advisable to start answering each question in turn. There may be anywhere from 50 to 100 such questions in the three or four hours allotted and you can see how much time would be taken if you read through all the questions before beginning to answer any. Furthermore, if you come across a question or group of questions which you know would be difficult to answer, it would undoubtedly affect your handling of all the other questions.

4) If the examination is of the essay type and contains but a few questions, it is a moot point as to whether you should read all the questions before starting to answer any one. Of course, if you are given a choice – say five out of seven and the like – then it is essential to read all the questions so you can eliminate the two that are most difficult. If, however, you are asked to answer all the questions, there may be danger in trying to answer the easiest one first because you may find that you will spend too much time on it. The best technique is to answer the first question, then proceed to the second, etc.

5) Time your answers. Before the exam begins, write down the time it started, then add the time allowed for the examination and write down the time it must be completed, then divide the time available somewhat as follows:
   - If 3-1/2 hours are allowed, that would be 210 minutes. If you have 80 objective-type questions, that would be an average of 2-1/2 minutes per question. Allow yourself no more than 2 minutes per question, or a total of 160 minutes, which will permit about 50 minutes to review.
   - If for the time allotment of 210 minutes there are 7 essay questions to answer, that would average about 30 minutes a question. Give yourself only 25 minutes per question so that you have about 35 minutes to review.

6) The most important instruction is to *read each question* and make sure you know what is wanted. The second most important instruction is to *time yourself properly* so that you answer every question. The third most important instruction is to *answer every question*. Guess if you have to but include something for each question. Remember that you will receive no credit for a blank and will probably receive some credit if you write something in answer to an essay question. If you guess a letter – say "B" for a multiple-choice question – you may have guessed right. If you leave a blank as an answer to a multiple-choice question, the examiners may respect your feelings but it will not add a point to your score. Some exams may penalize you for wrong answers, so in such cases *only*, you may not want to guess unless you have some basis for your answer.

7) Suggestions
   a. Objective-type questions
      1. Examine the question booklet for proper sequence of pages and questions
      2. Read all instructions carefully
      3. Skip any question which seems too difficult; return to it after all other questions have been answered
      4. Apportion your time properly; do not spend too much time on any single question or group of questions

5. Note and underline key words – *all, most, fewest, least, best, worst, same, opposite,* etc.
6. Pay particular attention to negatives
7. Note unusual option, e.g., unduly long, short, complex, different or similar in content to the body of the question
8. Observe the use of "hedging" words – *probably, may, most likely,* etc.
9. Make sure that your answer is put next to the same number as the question
10. Do not second-guess unless you have good reason to believe the second answer is definitely more correct
11. Cross out original answer if you decide another answer is more accurate; do not erase until you are ready to hand your paper in
12. Answer all questions; guess unless instructed otherwise
13. Leave time for review

   b. Essay questions
1. Read each question carefully
2. Determine exactly what is wanted. Underline key words or phrases.
3. Decide on outline or paragraph answer
4. Include many different points and elements unless asked to develop any one or two points or elements
5. Show impartiality by giving pros and cons unless directed to select one side only
6. Make and write down any assumptions you find necessary to answer the questions
7. Watch your English, grammar, punctuation and choice of words
8. Time your answers; don't crowd material

8) Answering the essay question

Most essay questions can be answered by framing the specific response around several key words or ideas. Here are a few such key words or ideas:

M's: manpower, materials, methods, money, management
P's: purpose, program, policy, plan, procedure, practice, problems, pitfalls, personnel, public relations

   a. Six basic steps in handling problems:
1. Preliminary plan and background development
2. Collect information, data and facts
3. Analyze and interpret information, data and facts
4. Analyze and develop solutions as well as make recommendations
5. Prepare report and sell recommendations
6. Install recommendations and follow up effectiveness

   b. Pitfalls to avoid
1. *Taking things for granted* – A statement of the situation does not necessarily imply that each of the elements is necessarily true; for example, a complaint may be invalid and biased so that all that can be taken for granted is that a complaint has been registered

2. *Considering only one side of a situation* – Wherever possible, indicate several alternatives and then point out the reasons you selected the best one
3. *Failing to indicate follow up* – Whenever your answer indicates action on your part, make certain that you will take proper follow-up action to see how successful your recommendations, procedures or actions turn out to be
4. *Taking too long in answering any single question* – Remember to time your answers properly

IX. AFTER THE TEST

Scoring procedures differ in detail among civil service jurisdictions although the general principles are the same. Whether the papers are hand-scored or graded by machine we have described, they are nearly always graded by number. That is, the person who marks the paper knows only the number – never the name – of the applicant. Not until all the papers have been graded will they be matched with names. If other tests, such as training and experience or oral interview ratings have been given, scores will be combined. Different parts of the examination usually have different weights. For example, the written test might count 60 percent of the final grade, and a rating of training and experience 40 percent. In many jurisdictions, veterans will have a certain number of points added to their grades.

After the final grade has been determined, the names are placed in grade order and an eligible list is established. There are various methods for resolving ties between those who get the same final grade – probably the most common is to place first the name of the person whose application was received first. Job offers are made from the eligible list in the order the names appear on it. You will be notified of your grade and your rank as soon as all these computations have been made. This will be done as rapidly as possible.

People who are found to meet the requirements in the announcement are called "eligibles." Their names are put on a list of eligible candidates. An eligible's chances of getting a job depend on how high he stands on this list and how fast agencies are filling jobs from the list.

When a job is to be filled from a list of eligibles, the agency asks for the names of people on the list of eligibles for that job. When the civil service commission receives this request, it sends to the agency the names of the three people highest on this list. Or, if the job to be filled has specialized requirements, the office sends the agency the names of the top three persons who meet these requirements from the general list.

The appointing officer makes a choice from among the three people whose names were sent to him. If the selected person accepts the appointment, the names of the others are put back on the list to be considered for future openings.

That is the rule in hiring from all kinds of eligible lists, whether they are for typist, carpenter, chemist, or something else. For every vacancy, the appointing officer has his choice of any one of the top three eligibles on the list. This explains why the person whose name is on top of the list sometimes does not get an appointment when some of the persons lower on the list do. If the appointing officer chooses the second or third eligible, the No. 1 eligible does not get a job at once, but stays on the list until he is appointed or the list is terminated.

X. HOW TO PASS THE INTERVIEW TEST

The examination for which you applied requires an oral interview test. You have already taken the written test and you are now being called for the interview test – the final part of the formal examination.

You may think that it is not possible to prepare for an interview test and that there are no procedures to follow during an interview. Our purpose is to point out some things you can do in advance that will help you and some good rules to follow and pitfalls to avoid while you are being interviewed.

What is an interview supposed to test?

The written examination is designed to test the technical knowledge and competence of the candidate; the oral is designed to evaluate intangible qualities, not readily measured otherwise, and to establish a list showing the relative fitness of each candidate – as measured against his competitors – for the position sought. Scoring is not on the basis of "right" and "wrong," but on a sliding scale of values ranging from "not passable" to "outstanding." As a matter of fact, it is possible to achieve a relatively low score without a single "incorrect" answer because of evident weakness in the qualities being measured.

Occasionally, an examination may consist entirely of an oral test – either an individual or a group oral. In such cases, information is sought concerning the technical knowledges and abilities of the candidate, since there has been no written examination for this purpose. More commonly, however, an oral test is used to supplement a written examination.

Who conducts interviews?

The composition of oral boards varies among different jurisdictions. In nearly all, a representative of the personnel department serves as chairman. One of the members of the board may be a representative of the department in which the candidate would work. In some cases, "outside experts" are used, and, frequently, a businessman or some other representative of the general public is asked to serve. Labor and management or other special groups may be represented. The aim is to secure the services of experts in the appropriate field.

However the board is composed, it is a good idea (and not at all improper or unethical) to ascertain in advance of the interview who the members are and what groups they represent. When you are introduced to them, you will have some idea of their backgrounds and interests, and at least you will not stutter and stammer over their names.

What should be done before the interview?

While knowledge about the board members is useful and takes some of the surprise element out of the interview, there is other preparation which is more substantive. It *is* possible to prepare for an oral interview – in several ways:

1) Keep a copy of your application and review it carefully before the interview

This may be the only document before the oral board, and the starting point of the interview. Know what education and experience you have listed there, and the sequence and dates of all of it. Sometimes the board will ask you to review the highlights of your experience for them; you should not have to hem and haw doing it.

2) Study the class specification and the examination announcement

Usually, the oral board has one or both of these to guide them. The qualities, characteristics or knowledges required by the position sought are stated in these documents. They offer valuable clues as to the nature of the oral interview. For example, if the job involves supervisory responsibilities, the announcement will usually indicate that knowledge of modern supervisory methods and the qualifications of the candidate as a supervisor will be tested. If so, you can expect such questions, frequently in the form of a hypothetical situation which you are expected to solve. NEVER go into an oral without knowledge of the duties and responsibilities of the job you seek.

3) Think through each qualification required

Try to visualize the kind of questions you would ask if you were a board member. How well could you answer them? Try especially to appraise your own knowledge and background in each area, *measured against the job sought*, and identify any areas in which you are weak. Be critical and realistic – do not flatter yourself.

4) Do some general reading in areas in which you feel you may be weak

For example, if the job involves supervision and your past experience has NOT, some general reading in supervisory methods and practices, particularly in the field of human relations, might be useful. Do NOT study agency procedures or detailed manuals. The oral board will be testing your understanding and capacity, not your memory.

5) Get a good night's sleep and watch your general health and mental attitude

You will want a clear head at the interview. Take care of a cold or any other minor ailment, and of course, no hangovers.

What should be done on the day of the interview?

Now comes the day of the interview itself. Give yourself plenty of time to get there. Plan to arrive somewhat ahead of the scheduled time, particularly if your appointment is in the fore part of the day. If a previous candidate fails to appear, the board might be ready for you a bit early. By early afternoon an oral board is almost invariably behind schedule if there are many candidates, and you may have to wait. Take along a book or magazine to read, or your application to review, but leave any extraneous material in the waiting room when you go in for your interview. In any event, relax and compose yourself.

The matter of dress is important. The board is forming impressions about you – from your experience, your manners, your attitude, and your appearance. Give your personal appearance careful attention. Dress your best, but not your flashiest. Choose conservative, appropriate clothing, and be sure it is immaculate. This is a business interview, and your appearance should indicate that you regard it as such. Besides, being well groomed and properly dressed will help boost your confidence.

Sooner or later, someone will call your name and escort you into the interview room. *This is it.* From here on you are on your own. It is too late for any more preparation. But remember, you asked for this opportunity to prove your fitness, and you are here because your request was granted.

What happens when you go in?

The usual sequence of events will be as follows: The clerk (who is often the board stenographer) will introduce you to the chairman of the oral board, who will introduce you to the other members of the board. Acknowledge the introductions before you sit down. Do not be surprised if you find a microphone facing you or a stenotypist sitting by. Oral interviews are usually recorded in the event of an appeal or other review.

Usually the chairman of the board will open the interview by reviewing the highlights of your education and work experience from your application – primarily for the benefit of the other members of the board, as well as to get the material into the record. Do not interrupt or comment unless there is an error or significant misinterpretation; if that is the case, do not hesitate. But do not quibble about insignificant matters. Also, he will usually ask you some question about your education, experience or your present job – partly to get you to start talking and to establish the interviewing "rapport." He may start the actual questioning, or turn it over to one of the other members. Frequently, each member undertakes the questioning on a particular area, one in which he is perhaps most competent, so you can expect each member to participate in the examination. Because time is limited, you may also expect some rather abrupt switches in the direction the questioning takes, so do not be upset by it. Normally, a board member will not pursue a single line of questioning unless he discovers a particular strength or weakness.

After each member has participated, the chairman will usually ask whether any member has any further questions, then will ask you if you have anything you wish to add. Unless you are expecting this question, it may floor you. Worse, it may start you off on an extended, extemporaneous speech. The board is not usually seeking more information. The question is principally to offer you a last opportunity to present further qualifications or to indicate that you have nothing to add. So, if you feel that a significant qualification or characteristic has been overlooked, it is proper to point it out in a sentence or so. Do not compliment the board on the thoroughness of their examination – they have been sketchy, and you know it. If you wish, merely say, "No thank you, I have nothing further to add." This is a point where you can "talk yourself out" of a good impression or fail to present an important bit of information. Remember, *you close the interview yourself*.

The chairman will then say, "That is all, Mr. _____, thank you." Do not be startled; the interview is over, and quicker than you think. Thank him, gather your belongings and take your leave. Save your sigh of relief for the other side of the door.

How to put your best foot forward

Throughout this entire process, you may feel that the board individually and collectively is trying to pierce your defenses, seek out your hidden weaknesses and embarrass and confuse you. Actually, this is not true. They are obliged to make an appraisal of your qualifications for the job you are seeking, and they want to see you in your best light. Remember, they must interview all candidates and a non-cooperative candidate may become a failure in spite of their best efforts to bring out his qualifications. Here are 15 suggestions that will help you:

1) Be natural – Keep your attitude confident, not cocky

If you are not confident that you can do the job, do not expect the board to be. Do not apologize for your weaknesses, try to bring out your strong points. The board is interested in a positive, not negative, presentation. Cockiness will antagonize any board member and make him wonder if you are covering up a weakness by a false show of strength.

2) Get comfortable, but don't lounge or sprawl

Sit erectly but not stiffly. A careless posture may lead the board to conclude that you are careless in other things, or at least that you are not impressed by the importance of the occasion. Either conclusion is natural, even if incorrect. Do not fuss with your clothing, a pencil or an ashtray. Your hands may occasionally be useful to emphasize a point; do not let them become a point of distraction.

3) Do not wisecrack or make small talk

This is a serious situation, and your attitude should show that you consider it as such. Further, the time of the board is limited – they do not want to waste it, and neither should you.

4) Do not exaggerate your experience or abilities

In the first place, from information in the application or other interviews and sources, the board may know more about you than you think. Secondly, you probably will not get away with it. An experienced board is rather adept at spotting such a situation, so do not take the chance.

5) If you know a board member, do not make a point of it, yet do not hide it

Certainly you are not fooling him, and probably not the other members of the board. Do not try to take advantage of your acquaintanceship – it will probably do you little good.

6) Do not dominate the interview

Let the board do that. They will give you the clues – do not assume that you have to do all the talking. Realize that the board has a number of questions to ask you, and do not try to take up all the interview time by showing off your extensive knowledge of the answer to the first one.

7) Be attentive

You only have 20 minutes or so, and you should keep your attention at its sharpest throughout. When a member is addressing a problem or question to you, give him your undivided attention. Address your reply principally to him, but do not exclude the other board members.

8) Do not interrupt

A board member may be stating a problem for you to analyze. He will ask you a question when the time comes. Let him state the problem, and wait for the question.

9) Make sure you understand the question

Do not try to answer until you are sure what the question is. If it is not clear, restate it in your own words or ask the board member to clarify it for you. However, do not haggle about minor elements.

10) Reply promptly but not hastily

A common entry on oral board rating sheets is "candidate responded readily," or "candidate hesitated in replies." Respond as promptly and quickly as you can, but do not jump to a hasty, ill-considered answer.

11) Do not be peremptory in your answers

A brief answer is proper – but do not fire your answer back. That is a losing game from your point of view. The board member can probably ask questions much faster than you can answer them.

12) Do not try to create the answer you think the board member wants

He is interested in what kind of mind you have and how it works – not in playing games. Furthermore, he can usually spot this practice and will actually grade you down on it.

13) Do not switch sides in your reply merely to agree with a board member

Frequently, a member will take a contrary position merely to draw you out and to see if you are willing and able to defend your point of view. Do not start a debate, yet do not surrender a good position. If a position is worth taking, it is worth defending.

14) Do not be afraid to admit an error in judgment if you are shown to be wrong

The board knows that you are forced to reply without any opportunity for careful consideration. Your answer may be demonstrably wrong. If so, admit it and get on with the interview.

15) Do not dwell at length on your present job

The opening question may relate to your present assignment. Answer the question but do not go into an extended discussion. You are being examined for a *new* job, not your present one. As a matter of fact, try to phrase ALL your answers in terms of the job for which you are being examined.

Basis of Rating

Probably you will forget most of these "do's" and "don'ts" when you walk into the oral interview room. Even remembering them all will not ensure you a passing grade. Perhaps you did not have the qualifications in the first place. But remembering them will help you to put your best foot forward, without treading on the toes of the board members.

Rumor and popular opinion to the contrary notwithstanding, an oral board wants you to make the best appearance possible. They know you are under pressure – but they also want to see how you respond to it as a guide to what your reaction would be under the pressures of the job you seek. They will be influenced by the degree of poise you display, the personal traits you show and the manner in which you respond.

ABOUT THIS BOOK

This book contains tests divided into Examination Sections. Go through each test, answering every question in the margin. We have also attached a sample answer sheet at the back of the book that can be removed and used. At the end of each test look at the answer key and check your answers. On the ones you got wrong, look at the right answer choice and learn. Do not fill in the answers first. Do not memorize the questions and answers, but understand the answer and principles involved. On your test, the questions will likely be different from the samples. Questions are changed and new ones added. If you understand these past questions you should have success with any changes that arise. Tests may consist of several types of questions. We have additional books on each subject should more study be advisable or necessary for you. Finally, the more you study, the better prepared you will be. This book is intended to be the last thing you study before you walk into the examination room. Prior study of relevant texts is also recommended. NLC publishes some of these in our Fundamental Series. Knowledge and good sense are important factors in passing your exam. Good luck also helps. So now study this Passbook, absorb the material contained within and take that knowledge into the examination. Then do your best to pass that exam.

EXAMINATION SECTION

EXAMINATION SECTION
TEST 1

DIRECTIONS: Each question or incomplete statement is followed by several suggested answers or completions. Select the one that *BEST* answers the question or completes the statement. *PRINT THE LETTER OF THE CORRECT ANSWER IN THE SPACE AT THE RIGHT.*

1. When 60,987 is added to 27,835, the result is 1._____
   A. 80,712   B. 80,822   C. 87,712   D. 88,822

2. The sum of 693 + 787 + 946 + 355 + 731 is 2._____
   A. 3,512   B. 3,502   C. 3,412   D. 3,402

3. When 2,586 is subtracted from 3,003, the result is 3._____
   A. 417   B. 527   C. 1,417   D. 1,527

4. When 1.32 is subtracted from 52.6, the result is 4._____
   A. 3.94   B. 5.128   C. 39.4   D. 51.28

5. When 56 is multiplied by 438, the result is 5._____
   A. 840   B. 4,818   C. 24,528   D. 48,180

6. When 8.7 is multiplied by .34, the result is, most nearly, 6._____
   A. 2.9   B. 3.0   C. 29.5   D. 29.6

7. When 1/2 is divided by 2/3, the result is 7._____
   A. 1/3   B. 3/4   C. 1 1/3   D. 3

8. When 8,340 is divided by 38, the result is, most nearly 8._____
   A. 210   B. 218   C. 219   D. 220

Questions 9-11.

DIRECTIONS: Questions 9 to 11 inclusive are to be answered *SOLELY* on the basis of the information given below.

Assume that a certain water treatment plant has consumed quantities of chemicals E and F over a five-week period, as indicated in the following table:

Time Period	Number of 100-pound sacks consumed	
	Chemical E	Chemical F
Week 1	5	4
Week 2	7	5
Week 3	6	5
Week 4	8	6
Week 5	6	4

9. The *total* number of pounds of chemical E consumed at the end of the first three weeks is

   A. 180   B. 320   C. 1,400   D. 1,800

10. According to the table, the week in which the *most* chemicals were consumed was

    A. week 2   B. week 3   C. week 4   D. week 5

11. According to the table, the *average* number of sacks of chemical F consumed over the first four weeks was

    A. 4   B. 5   C. 6   D. 7

12. Of the following actions, the *best* one to take FIRST after smoke is seen coming from an electric control device is to

    A. shut off the power to it
    B. call the main office for advice
    C. look for a wiring diagram
    D. throw water on it

13. Of the following items, the one which would LEAST likely be included on a memorandum is the

    A. home address of the writer of the memorandum
    B. name of the writer of the memorandum
    C. subject of the memorandum
    D. names or titles of the person who will receive the memorandum

14. When testing joints for leaks in pipe lines containing natural gas, it is BEST to use

    A. water in the lines under pressure
    B. a lighted candle
    C. an aquastat
    D. soapy water

Questions 15-17.

DIRECTIONS: Questions 15 to 17 inclusive are to be answered SOLELY on the basis of the information given below.

Assume that at various hours of a typical day the amounts of chlorine residual in parts per million (ppm) at a certain water treatment plant are as shown in the following graph:

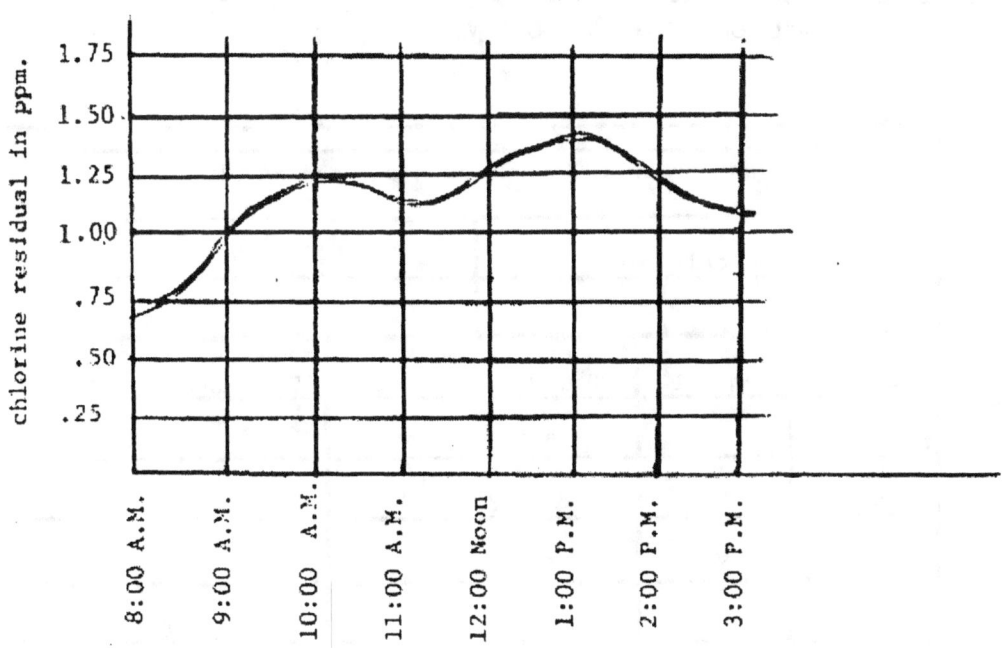

15. According to the graph, the chlorine residual measured in ppm at 9:00 A.M. was, most nearly,

    A. .70   B. .75   C. 1.00   D. 1.25

16. The maximum chlorine residual between 8:00 A.M. and 3:00 P.M. was, most nearly,

    A. .68 ppm   B. 1.10 ppm   C. 1.25 ppm   D. 1.37 ppm

17. According to the graph, between the hour of 12:00 Noon and 1:00 P.M., the chlorine residual was

    A. always increasing
    B. always decreasing
    C. increasing, then decreasing
    D. decreasing, then increasing

18. Of the following statements concerning the use and care of wooden ladders, the *one* which is *TRUE* is that

    A. a light oil should be applied to the rungs to preserve the wood
    B. each rung should be sharply struck with a metal hammer to test its soundness before using it
    C. ladders should be stored in a warm damp area to prevent the wood from getting brittle
    D. tops of ordinary stepladders should not be used as steps

19. It is *poor* practice to use gasoline to clean metal parts that are coated with grease *PRIMARILY* because gasoline

    A. contains lead which is harmful to the user
    B. is a poor solvent for grease
    C. corrodes metal
    D. vapors ignite easily

Questions 20-21.

DIRECTIONS: Questions 20 and 21 are to be answered SOLELY on the basis of the information given in the tables below.

Inventory of 100 pound bags on hand as of 1-1	
Chemical X	16 1/2
Chemical Y	12

Date	Chemical	Number of 100 pound bags used	Number of 100 pound bags received
1-5	X	8 1/2	
1-9	X	3 1/2	
1-9	Y	5	
1-14	X		8
1-18	Y	2 1/2	
1-23	X	3	
1-27	Y	4 1/2	
1-30	X		2
1-31	X	1	

Inventory of 100 pound bags on hand as of 1-31	
Chemical X	
Chemical Y	

J. Doe
Operator

2-2

20. According to the information given in the table, the number of 100-pound bags of chemical Y *on hand* as of 1-31 is

    A. 0   B. 1/2   C. 1   D. 1 1/2

20.___

21. According to the information in the table, the *total* number of pounds of chemical X consumed in the month was, most nearly,

    A. 500   B. 1,600   C. 1,800   D. 2,800

21.___

Questions 22-27.

DIRECTIONS: Questions 22 to 27 inclusive are to be answered *SOLELY* on the basis of the paragraph below.

FIRST AID INSTRUCTIONS

The main purpose of first aid is to put the injured person in the best possible position until medical help arrives. This includes the performance of emergency treatment for the purpose of saving a life if a doctor is not present. When a person is hurt, a crowd usually gathers around the victim. If nobody uses his head, the injured person fails to get the care he needs. You must stay calm and, most important, it is your duty to take charge at an accident. The first thing for you to do is to see, as best you can, what is wrong with the injured person. Leave the victim where he is until the nature and extent of his injury are determined. If he is unconscious he should not be moved except to lay him flat on his back if he is in some other position. Loosen the clothing of any seriously hurt person and make him as comfortable as possible. Medical help should be called as soon as possible. You should remain with the injured person and send someone else to call the doctor. You should try to make sure that the one who calls for a doctor is able to give correct information as to the location of the injured person. In order to help the physician to know what equipment may be needed in each particular case, the person making the call should give the doctor as much information about the injury as possible.

22. If nobody uses his head at the scene of an accident, there is danger that

    A. no one will get the names of all the witnesses
    B. a large crowd will gather
    C. the victim will not get the care he needs
    D. the victim will blame the City for negligence

22._____

23. When an accident occurs, the *FIRST* thing you should do is

    A. call a doctor
    B. loosen the clothing of the injured person
    C. notify the victim's family
    D. try to find out what is wrong with the injured person

23._____

24. If you do *NOT* know the extent and nature of the victim's injuries, you should

    A. let the injured person lie where he is
    B. immediately take the victim to a hospital yourself
    C. help the injured person to his feet to see if he can walk
    D. have the injured person sit up on the ground while you examine him

24._____

25. If the injured person is breathing and unconscious, you should

    A. get some hot liquid such as coffee or tea in to him
    B. give him artificial respiration
    C. lift up his head to try to stimulate blood circulation
    D. see that he lies flat on his back

25._____

26. If it is necessary to call a doctor, you should

    A. go and make the call yourself since you have all the information
    B. find out who the victim's family doctor is before making the call
    C. have someone else make the call who knows the location of the victim
    D. find out which doctor the victim can afford

27. It is important for the caller to give the doctor as much information as is available regarding the injury so that the doctor

    A. can bring the necessary equipment
    B. can make out an accident report
    C. will be responsible for any malpractice resulting from the first aid treatment
    D. can inform his nurse on how long he will be in the field

Questions 28-29.

DIRECTIONS: Questions 28 and 29 are to be answered *SOLELY* on the basis of the paragraph below.

When a written report must be submitted by an operator to his supervisor, the best rule is "the briefer the better." Obviously, this can be carried to extremes, since all necessary information must be included. However, the ability to write a satisfactory one-page report is an important communication skill. There are several different kinds of reports in common use. One is the form report, which is printed and merely requires the operator to fill in blanks. The greatest problems faced in completion of this report are accuracy and thoroughness. Another type of report is one that must be submitted regularly and systematically. This type of report is known as the periodic report.

28. According to the passage above, accuracy and thoroughness are the *GREATEST* problems in the completion of

    A. one-page reports B. form reports
    C. periodic reports D. long reports

29. According to the passage above, a good written report from an operator to his supervisor should be

    A. printed
    B. formal
    C. periodic
    D. brief

Question 30.

DIRECTIONS: The sketches below show 150-lb. chlorine cylinders stored in three different ways:

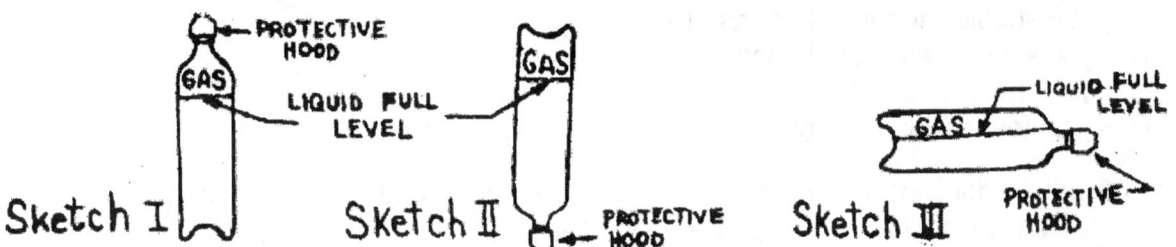

30. *Recommended* practice is to store a 150-lb. chlorine cylinder as shown in

    A. Sketch I *only*
    B. Sketch II *only*
    C. Sketch III *only*
    D. Sketches II and III

31. Of the following, the MOST serious defect in the installation shown below is that

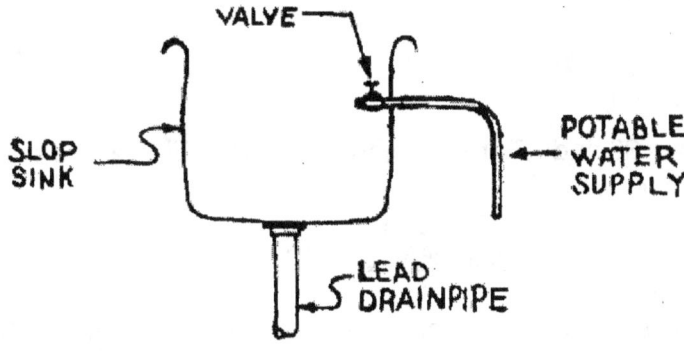

   A. the water supply should be directed downward to prevent excessive splashing over the rim
   B. the above installation may allow backflow of waste water into the water supply line
   C. lead pipes should not be used on drains from fixtures connected to the potable water supply
   D. excessive corrosion will occur on the valve if it becomes submerged

32. Of the following, the distance "x" which would be SAFEST when using the extension ladder shown in the sketch below is

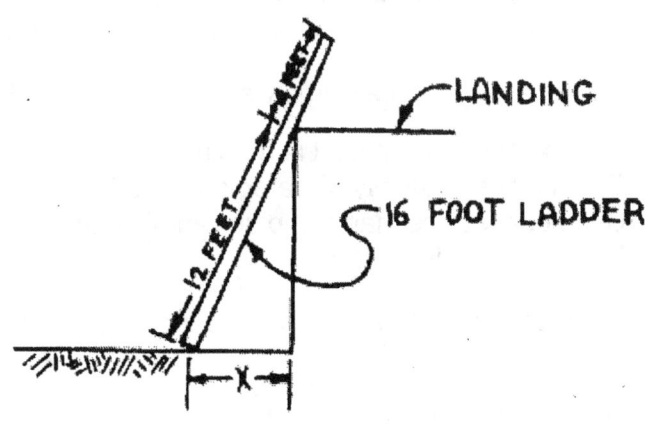

   A. 1 foot   B. 3 feet   C. 5 feet   D. 7 fee

33. Of the following statements regarding safe procedures for lifting a heavy object by yourself from the floor, the one which is FALSE is that   33.____

    A. you should keep your back as straight as possible
    B. you should bend your knees
    C. you should mainly use your back muscles in lifting
    D. your feet should be kept clear in case the object is dropped

34. It is generally not considered to be good practice to paint wood ladders. Of the following, the *best* reason for *NOT* painting wood ladders is that   34.____

    A. it may hide defects in the wood
    B. the rungs become slippery
    C. the hardware on the ladder becomes unworkable
    D. it would rub off on the surfaces against which it is resting

35. A rip saw would *MOST* likely be used to cut   35.____

    A. wood   B. steel   C. copper   D. aluminum

Questions 36-37.

DIRECTIONS: Questions 36 and 37 are to be answered *SOLELY* on the basis of the paragraph below.

NATURAL LAKES

Large lakes may yield water of exceptionally fine quality except near the shore line and in the vicinity of sewer outlets or near outlets of large streams. Therefore, minimum treatment is required. The availability of practically unlimited quantities of water is also a decided advantage. Unfortunately, however, the sewage from a city is often discharged into the same lake from which the water supply is taken. Great care must be taken in locating both the water intake and the sewer outlet so that the pollution handled by the water treatment plant is a minimum.

Sometimes the distance from the shore where dependable, satisfactory water can be found is so great that the cost of water intake facilities is prohibitive for a small municipality. In such cases, another supply must be found, or water must be obtained from a neighboring large city. Lake water is usually uniform in quality from day to day and does not vary in temperature as much as water from a river or small impounding reservoir.

36. A disadvantage of drawing a water supply from a large lake is that   36.____

    A. expensive treatment is required
    B. a limited quantity of water is available
    C. nearby cities may dump sewage into the lake
    D. the water is too cold.

37. An advantage of drawing a water supply from a large lake is that the   37.____

    A. water is uniform in quality
    B. water varies in temperature
    C. intake is distant from the shore
    D. intake may be near a sewer outlet

38. The *BEST* type of wrench to use to tighten a pipe without marring the pipe surface is   38.____

    A. pipe wrench
    B. strap wrench
    C. spanner wrench
    D. box wrench

39. Of the following statements concerning the use and care of files, the *one* which is *FALSE*   39.____
    is that

    A. files should have tight-fitting handles
    B. rasps are generally used on wood
    C. files should be protected by a light coating of oil when cutting metal
    D. files should be given a quick blow on a wood block to unclog teeth

40. A device which permits flow of a fluid in a pipe in one direction only is known as   40.____

    A. diode
    B. curb box
    C. gooseneck
    D. check valve

KEY (CORRECT ANSWERS)

1.	D	11.	B	21.	B	31.	B
2.	A	12.	A	22.	C	32.	B
3.	A	13.	A	23.	D	33.	C
4.	D	14.	D	24.	A	34.	A
5.	C	15.	C	25.	D	35.	A
6.	B	16.	D	26.	C	36.	C
7.	B	17.	A	27.	A	37.	A
8.	C	18.	D	28.	B	38.	B
9.	D	19.	D	29.	D	39.	C
10.	C	20.	A	30.	A	40.	D

TEST 2

DIRECTIONS: Each question or incomplete statement is followed by several suggested answers or completions. Select the one that *BEST* answers the question or completes the statement. *PRINT THE LETTER OF THE CORRECT ANSWER IN THE SPACE AT THE RIGHT.*

Questions 1-2.

DIRECTIONS: Questions 1 and 2 are to be answered *SOLELY* on the basis of the paragraph below.

PRECIPITATION AND RUNOFF

In the United States, the average annual precipitation is about 30 inches, of which about 21 inches is lost to the atmosphere by evaporation and transpiration. The remaining 9 inches becomes runoff into rivers and lakes. Both the precipitation and runoff vary greatly with geography and season. Annual precipitation varies from more than 100 inches in parts of the northwest to only 2 or 3 inches in parts of the southwest. In the northeastern part of the country, including New York State, the annual average precipitation is about 45 inches, of which about 22 inches becomes runoff. Even in New York State, there is some variation from place to place and considerable variation from time to time. During extremely dry years, the precipitation may be as low as 30 inches and the runoff below 10 inches. In general, there are greater variations in runoff rates from smaller watersheds. A critical water supply situation occurs when there are three or four abnormally dry years in succession.

Precipitation over the state is measured and recorded by a net- work of stations operated by the U. S. Weather Bureau. All of the precipitation records and other data such as temperature, humidity and evaporation rates are published monthly by the Weather Bureau in "Climatological Data." Runoff rates at more than 200 stream-gauging stations in the state are measured and recorded by the U. S. Geological Survey in cooperation with various state agencies. Records of the daily average flows are published annually by the U. S. Geological Survey in "Surface Water Records of New York." Copies may be obtained by writing to the Water Resources Division, United States Geological Survey, Albany, New York 23301.

1. From the above paragraphs it is *appropriate* to conclude that

   A. critical supply situations do not occur
   B. the greater the rainfall, the greater the runoff
   C. there are greater variations in runoff from larger watersheds
   D. the rainfall in the southwest is greater than the average in the country

2. From the above paragraphs, it is appropriate to conclude that

   A. an annual rainfall of about 50 inches does not occur in New York State
   B. the U. S. Weather Bureau is only interested in rainfall
   C. runoff is equal to rainfall less losses to the atmosphere
   D. information about rainfall and runoff in New York State is unavailable to the public

2 (#2)

3. The following are diagrams of various types of bolt heads.

   The *one* of the above which is a Phillips head type is the one labelled
   A. A   B. B   C. C   D. D

4. The appearance of frost on the outer surface of a chlorine cylinder which has been placed in service would MOST likely indicate that

   A. the cylinder is empty
   B. the gas is escaping too quickly from the cylinder
   C. there is too much pressure in the cylinder
   D. the humidity of the storage area is too high

5. One of the outer belts of a matched set of three V-belts becomes badly frayed. Of the following, the BEST course of action to take is to

   A. replace only the worn belt
   B. replace only the worn belt but put the new belt in the middle
   C. remove the worn belt, put the center belt on the end and continue running the machine
   D. replace the whole set of belts even if the other two belts show no signs of wear\

6. Of the following, the BEST type of valve to use for throttling or when the valve must be opened and closed frequently is a

   A. check valve   B. globe valve
   C. butterfly valve   D. pop valve

7. Of the following, the device which is used to measure *both* pressure and vacuum is the

   A. compound gage   B. aquastat
   C. pyrometer   D. thermocouple

8. Electrical energy is consumed and paid for in units of

   A. voltage   B. ampere-hours
   C. kilowatt-hours   D. watts

9. A "governor" on an engine is used to control the engine's

   A. speed   B. temperature
   C. interval of operation
   D. engaging and disengaging the "load"

10. Pressure *below* that of the atmospheric pressure is usually expressed in

    A. vacuum inches of mercury   B. inches of pressure absolute
    C. BTU's   D. gallons per minute

11. A short piece of pipe with outside threads at both ends is called a

   A. union B. nipple C. tee D. sleeve

12. Of the following, which device would MOST likely produce water hammer in a plumbing installation? A(n)

   A. relief valve
   B. air chamber
   C. surge tank
   D. quick-closing valve

13. Some portable electric tools have a third conductor in the line cord which is electrically connected to the receptacle box. The reason for this is to

   A. have a spare wire in case one power wire breaks
   B. protect the user of the tool from electrical shock
   C. strengthen the power lead so that it cannot be easily damaged
   D. allow use of the tool for extended periods of time without overheating

14. Of the following, the device which is usually used to measure the rate of flow of water in a pipe is a

   A. pressure gage
   B. Bourden gage
   C. manometer
   D. velocity meter

15. Acid, rosin fluid, or paste applied to metal surfaces to remove oxide film in preparation for soldering is known as

   A. grout B. lampblack C. plumber's soil D. flux

16. In plumbing work, a coil spring which is inserted into a drain to facilitate cleaning of the drain is known as a

   A. pipe reamer B. snake C. plunger D. spigot

17. Of the following, a pneumatic device is one that is driven or powered by

   A. air pressure
   B. oil pressure
   C. water pressure
   D. steam pressure

18. Of the following metals, the one which would MOST likely be used for an electric motor shaft is

   A. wrought iron
   B. hard bronze
   C. steel
   D. bras

19. Of the following, a rotary gear pump is BEST suited for pumping

   A. #6 fuel oil B. hot water C. sewage D. kerosene

20. The MAIN reason for using a flexible coupling to join the shafts of two pieces of machinery together is that a flexible coupling

   A. allows for slight misalignment of the two shafts
   B. can be immediately disengaged in an emergency
   C. will automatically slip when overloaded thus protecting the driver machinery
   D. allows the driven load shaft to continue rotating under its own momentum, when the driver shaft is stopped

21. Of the following, the MAIN purpose of a house trap is to

    A. provide the house drain with a cleanout
    B. prevent gases from the public sewer from entering the house plumbing system
    C. trap articles of value that are accidentally dropped into the drainage pipes
    D. eliminate the necessity for traps under all other plumbing fixtures

22. Of the following, the MAIN reason for sometimes applying bituminous coating to the interiors of steel and cast-iron pipe is that this coating

    A. increases the tensile strength of the pipe
    B. increases the shock resistance of the pipe
    C. removes any objectionable taste from the water imparted by the pipe walls
    D. protects the pipe walls from corrosion

23. The one of the following electrical devices which is most likely to be used to raise or lower A.C. voltages is a

    A. resistor   B. thermistor   C. transformer   D. circuit-breaker

24. When a metal is galvanized, it is given a coating of

    A. nickel   B. tin   C. oxide   D. zinc

25. A conduit hickey is used to

    A. measure conduit pipe   B. bend conduit pipe
    C. thread conduit pipe   D. cut conduit pipe

Questions 26-27.

   DIRECTIONS: Questions 26 and 27 are to be answered SOLELY on the basis of the electrical circuit shown below.

26. The circuit above is commonly known as a

    A. series circuit   B. parallel circuit
    C. short circuit   D. circuit breaker

27. The current flowing in the circuit above is

    A. 1 amp   B. 2 amps   C. 3 amps   D. 6 amps

Questions 28-30.

DIRECTIONS: Questions 28 to 30 inclusive are to be answered SOLELY on the basis of the sketches shown below.

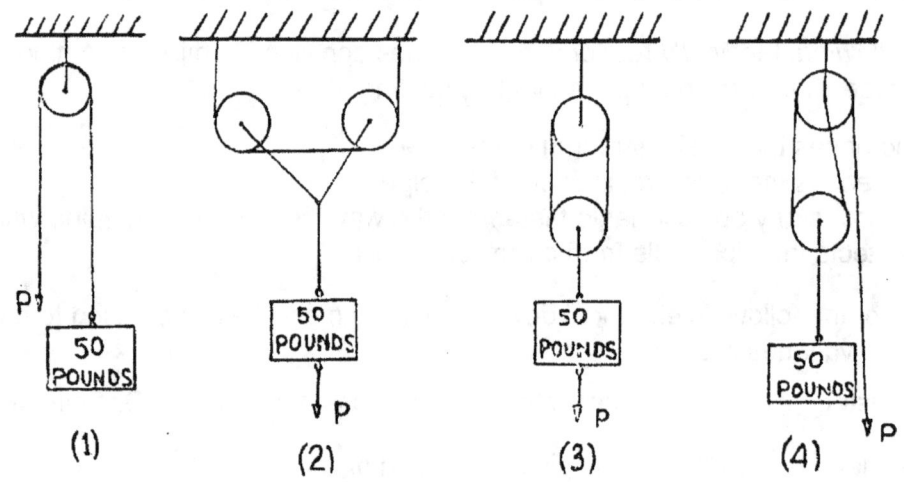

28. The two arrangements in the above diagrams which CANNOT be used to raise the load at all by applying a pull "p" as shown are setups

    A. 1 and 2   B. 2 and 3   C. 3 and 4   D. 1 and 4

29. The arrangement in the diagram above which requires the LEAST effort "p" to move the 50-pound weight is setup

    A. 1   B. 2   C. 3   D. 4

30. The effort required to hold the 50-pound weight at rest off the ground in setup (1) in the diagram above is

    A. 10 pounds   B. 25 pounds   C. 50 pounds   D. 100 pounds

31. Of the following formulas, the one which CORRECTLY shows the relationship between gage pressure and absolute pressure is

    A. Absolute pressure = gage pressure / atmospheric pressure
    B. Absolute pressure + gage pressure = atmospheric pressure
    C. Absolute pressure = gage pressure + atmospheric pressure
    D. Absolute pressure + atmospheric pressure = gage pressure

32. The weight of a gallon of water is, most nearly,

    A. 8.3 pounds   B. 16.6 pounds   C. 24.9 pounds   D. 33.2 pounds

33. Solenoid valves are usually operated

    A. thermally   B. manually   C. hydraulically   D. electrically

34. A 1/2-inch, 8-32 round-head machine screw has

    A. a diameter of 1/2 inch
    B. a length of 8 inches
    C. 8 threads per inch
    D. 32 threads per inch

35. The MAIN purpose for the stuffing usually found in centrifugal pump stuffing boxes is

    A. supporting the shaft
    B. controlling the rate of discharge
    C. preventing fluid leakage
    D. compensating for shaft misalignment

36. The BEST wrench to use on screwed valves and fittings having hexagonal shape connections is the

    A. chain wrench
    B. open-end wrench
    C. pipe wrench
    D. strap wrench

37. A tap is a tool commonly used to

    A. remove broken screws
    B. flare pipe ends
    C. cut external threads
    D. cut internal threads

38. A thread chaser is MOST likely to be used to

    A. rethread damaged threads
    B. remove broken taps
    C. flare tubing
    D. adjust diestocks

39. If an air-conditioning unit shorted out and caught fire, the BEST fire extinguisher to use would be a

    A. water extinguisher
    B. foam extinguisher
    C. carbon dioxide extinguisher
    D. soda acid extinguisher

40. Of the following, the best action to take to help someone whose eyes have been splashed with lye is to FIRST

    A. wash out the eyes with clean water
    B. wash out the eyes with a salt water solution
    C. apply a sterile dressing over the eyes
    D. do nothing to the eyes, but telephone for medical help

KEY (CORRECT ANSWERS)

1.	B	11.	B	21.	B	31.	C
2.	C	12.	D	22.	D	32.	A
3.	C	13.	B	23.	C	33.	D
4.	B	14.	D	24.	D	34.	D
5.	D	15.	D	25.	B	35.	C
6.	B	16.	B	26.	A	36.	B
7.	A	17.	A	27.	B	37.	D
8.	C	18.	C	28.	B	38.	A
9.	A	19.	A	29.	D	39.	C
10.	A	20.	A	30.	C	40.	A

EXAMINATION SECTION
TEST 1

DIRECTIONS: Each question or incomplete statement is followed by several suggested answers or completions. Select the one the BEST answers the question or completes the statement. *PRINT THE LETTER OF THE CORRECT ANSWER IN THE SPACE AT THE RIGHT.*

1. Potential contaminants of drinking water as a consequence of disinfection treatment include each of the following, EXCEPT

    A. Hypochlorous acid
    B. Chlorite
    C. Chlorine dioxide
    D. Chloramine

    1.____

2. Substances applied in the pretreatment of raw water that has undergone eutrophication typically include
    I. Sodium phosphate
    II. Sodium thiosulphate
    III. Chlorine
    IV. Copper sulfate

    A. I and II
    B. II and III
    C. III and IV
    D. I, II, III and IV

    2.____

3. Which of the following processes typically occurs EARLIEST in the water treatment sequence?

    A. Direct filtration
    B. Fluoridation
    C. Chlorination
    D. Disinfection

    3.____

4. The major inconvenience of prolonged pre-treatment storage in an artificial tank or reservoir is

    A. excessive turbidity
    B. eutrophication
    C. the accumulation of sludge
    D. the loss of dissolved oxygen

    4.____

5. The large majority of public water systems will register a pH that is

    A. absolutely neutral
    B. slightly basic
    C. slightly acid
    D. moderately acid

    5.____

17

6. The most reliable absorber of synthetic organic chemicals in water is

   A. sodium thiosulfate
   B. activated carbon
   C. silica gel
   D. activated alumina

7. Which of the following contaminants is classified as a primary drinking water standard by the EPA?

   A. Coliform group
   B. Foaming agents
   C. Total dissolved solids
   D. Corrosivity

8. Typically, the temperature of water sampled for an Odor Threshold Test should be between _____ °C.

   A. 10-15
   B. 25-40
   C. 40-60
   D. 65-85

9. Which of the following types of water analyses requires the largest sample volume?

   A. Biological oxygen demand (BOD)
   B. pH
   C. Chlorine
   D. Total solids

10. A _____ solution of an acid is one that contains 1.008 gram of replaceable hydrogen in one liter of solution.

    A. saturated
    B. molar
    C. supersaturated
    D. normal

11. Which of the following chemicals has been assigned a maximum contaminant level (MCL) by the EPA?

    A. Molybdenum
    B. Aluminum
    C. Sodium
    D. Zinc

12. At low turbidity levels, the most efficient viral removal treatment is

    A. coagulation/flocculation
    B. filtration
    C. settling
    D. disinfection

13. Which of the following compounds would contribute to the "temporary hardness" of water?

    A. Magnesium carbonate
    B. Sodium bicarbonate
    C. Potassium carbonate
    D. Calcium chloride

14. Which of the following coagulants may be objectionable in a distribution system, due to problems with steam boilers?

    A. Calcite or whiting
    B. Liquid alum
    C. Quicklime
    D. Activated silica

15. Which of the following is named by the EPA as the best available technology for removing fluoride?

    A. Electrodialysis
    B. Anion exchange resins
    C. Modified lime softening
    D. Activated alumina adsorption

16. For rapid sand filtration, the minimum filtration rate should be set at about _____ gal/sq.ft/min.

    A. 2
    B. 20
    C. 35
    D. 80

17. The liquid chromatographic post-column fluorescence method, according to Standard Methods, is an acceptable analysis for detecting the presence of

    A. extractable base/neutrals and acids
    B. volatile halocarbons
    C. polynuclear aromatic hydrocarbons
    D. glyphosate herbicides

18. The data on a plant's inventory cards typically include
    I. equipment inventory numbers
    II. equipment schedule numbers
    III. maintenance schedules
    IV. any maintenance work orders or reports

    A. I and II
    B. I and III
    C. II, III and IV
    D. I, II, III and IV

19. Which of the following is a volatile organic compound?

    A. Vinyl chloride
    B. Carbolic acid
    C. Toluene
    D. Atrazine

20. The most effective methods for removing arsenic from drinking water include each of the following, EXCEPT

    A. activated aluminum
    B. coagulation with filtration
    C. ion exchange
    D. electrodialysis

21. Typically, the minimum detention time required for the settling process is _____ hour(s).

    A. 1
    B. 2
    C. 4
    D. 6

22. Which of the following is a base monitoring requirement for trihalomethanes (THMs)?

    A. In the system, a minimum of 50% of samples taken at the maximum residence time
    B. In the system, 50% of samples taken at named representative locations
    C. A minimum of 4 samples per quarter at treatment plants
    D. A minimum of 1 sample per quarter at treatment plants

23. What is the EPA's maximum contaminant level (MCL, in mg/L) for selenium?

    A. 0.005
    B. 0.050
    C. 0.500
    D. 5.000

24. "Breakpoint" is a term that applies to the process of

    A. Coagulation/flocculation
    B. Fluoridation
    C. Ion exchange
    D. Chlorination

25. For soft waters, the pH range generally required for best coagulation results is about

    A. 5.2-6.0
    B. 5.8-6.4
    C. 6.8-7.8
    D. 7.2-8.0

KEY (CORRECT ANSWERS)

1. A
2. C
3. C
4. C
5. B

6. B
7. A
8. C
9. A
10. D

11. A
12. D
13. A
14. D
15. D

16. A
17. D
18. A
19. A
20. B

21. C
22. C
23. B
24. D
25. B

TEST 2

DIRECTIONS: Each question or incomplete statement is followed by several suggested answers or completions. Select the one the BEST answers the question or completes the statement. *PRINT THE LETTER OF THE CORRECT ANSWER IN THE SPACE AT THE RIGHT.*

1. Which of the following traditional treatment processes is most effective at removing volatile compounds?   1.___

    A. Chlorination
    B. Activated carbon treatment
    C. Coagulation
    D. Aeration

2. Which of the following is classified as a chemical treatment?   2.___

    A. Coagulation
    B. Water softening
    C. Diatomaceous filtration
    D. Activated carbon treatment

3. Factors which influence the surface load of a sedimentation basin include   3.___
    I. depth
    II. width
    III. flow
    IV. length

    A. I, II and IV
    B. I and III
    C. II and IV
    D. I, II, III and IV

4. Major goals of removing settleable particles from raw waters include the reduction of each of the following, EXCEPT   4.___

    A. hardness
    B. turbidity
    C. color
    D. pH

5. Of the following, which complaint is most often reported by consumers of drinking water?   5.___

    A. Fishy odor
    B. Cloudy appearance
    C. Chlorine taste
    D. Off-color appearance

6. Pretreatment storage in an artificial tank is particularly effective when raw water is derived from a(n)   6.___

    A. lake   B. river   C. aquifer   D. well

7. Under the Safe Drinking Water Act, the minimum and maximum allowable pH range for potability is   7.____

   A. 4-9
   B. 5.5-8.6
   C. 6.5 - 8.5
   D. 7.0 - 7.8

8. Of the following treatments, which would normally be selected for organic contaminants?   8.____

   A. Ion exchange
   B. Activated alumina
   C. Reverse osmosis
   D. Packed-tower aeration

9. Which of the following inorganic chemicals is LEAST likely to appear in a drinking water supply?   9.____

   A. Sulfate
   B. Zinc
   C. Aluminum
   D. Nickel

10. Oxygen's content in water is approximately _____% of the dissolved gases.   10.____

    A. 17
    B. 38
    C. 54
    D. 72

11. Advantages of hard water over soft water generally include   11.____
    I. Less likely to produce scale in hot water pipes and heaters
    II. Less danger of corrosivity
    III. Better taste

    A. I only
    B. I and II
    C. II and III
    D. I, II and III

12. Flocs are removed from water by the process of   12.____

    A. filtration
    B. coagulation
    C. disinfection
    D. sedimentation

13. When no other raw water source is available and hardness is at or above _____ ppm, softening should be considered.

    A. 50
    B. 100
    C. 150
    D. 200

14. Each of the following assumptions can be considered reasonable in the calculation of the Accepted Daily Intake (ADI) or Adjusted Acceptable Daily Intake (AADI) of a chemical or compound, EXCEPT

    A. The target of the acceptable daily intake is the Suggested No-Adverse-Response-Level (SNARL)
    B. When insufficient data are available for air and food contamination, a 20% contribution from drinking water is typically used in preparing standards
    C. Water intake used in formulas is of 2 liters (2.11 quarts) per day
    D. An adult of 70 kg (154 lb.) is computed in health-related formulas

15. Packed-tower stripping is the only EPA-named "best available technology" for the removal of

    A. benzene
    B. vinyl chloride
    C. asbestos
    D. dioxin

16. In general, the treatment period required for flocculation is about

    A. 5-10 minutes
    B. 10-30 minutes
    C. 30-60 minutes
    D. 1-2 hours

17. In nature, mercury occurs rarely in a free state, but usually in combination with

    A. silver
    B. sulfur
    C. iron
    D. oxygen

18. According to Standard Methods, which of the following tests is appropriate method of analysis for carbamate pesticides?

    A. High performance liquid chromatography
    B. Purge-and-trap capillary column gas chromatography
    C. Purge-and-trap mass spectrometry
    D. Volumetric method

19. Which of the following is LEAST likely to occur as a waterborne disease?

    A. Typhoid
    B. Cholera
    C. Infectious hepatitis
    D. Diarrhea/enteritis

4 (#2)

20. In order to assure proper functioning of the retention tank and auxiliary pumping components, it is important for a dissolved air flotation (DAF) system to be operated between the design pressure specifications of _____ psi.   20._____

   A. 10-20
   B. 25-50
   C. 40-90
   D. 75-120

21. In the International System of Units (SI), which of the following is the unit of absolute viscosity?   21._____

   A. Stoke
   B. Brix
   C. Poise
   D. Gill

22. For raw waters high in color, the pH range generally required for best coagulation results is about   22._____

   A. 5.0-6.0
   B. 5.8-6.4
   C. 6.8-7.8
   D. 7.0-8.0

23. Which of the following is a Class A carcinogen, as classified by the EPA?   23._____

   A. Arsenic
   B. Cadmium
   C. PCBs
   D. Toluene

24. Which of the following types of water analyses requires the shortest maximum holding time?   24._____

   A. Phenolics
   B. Organic carbon
   C. Turbidity
   D. pH

25. Water depth over the filtration media should be maintained at about _____ feet.   25._____

   A. 4-5
   B. 7-10
   C. 12-16
   D. 18-25

KEY (CORRECT ANSWERS)

1. D
2. B
3. D
4. D
5. C

6. B
7. C
8. D
9. C
10. B

11. C
12. A
13. C
14. A
15. B

16. B
17. B
18. A
19. C
20. C

21. C
22. A
23. A
24. D
25. A

TEST 3

DIRECTIONS: Each question or incomplete statement is followed by several suggested answers or completions. Select the one the BEST answers the question or completes the statement. *PRINT THE LETTER OF THE CORRECT ANSWER IN THE SPACE AT THE RIGHT.*

1. Which of the following is NOT typically included in the operational record of a water treatment plant?

    A. Units not in service
    B. Time of coagulant application
    C. Quantity of chemicals used in treatment
    D. Time of sampling

    1.____

2. The desirable upper limit of total solids in a public water supply is _____mg/L.

    A. 150
    B. 500
    C. 750
    D. 1000

    2.____

3. Which of the following is a disadvantage associated with chlorination at several points from intake to distribution?

    A. Ineffective bactericidal treatment
    B. Inability to adapt to a sudden deterioration of quality
    C. High dosage requirements
    D. Complexity of construction

    3.____

4. Under the EPA's Phase II rules, sampling for synthetic organic compounds must occur

    A. once, during the first year only
    B. once each year for surface water and once every three years for groundwater
    C. quarterly for the first year, annually after that, and then every 3 years if not detected
    D. once for four consecutive quarters

    4.____

5. In industrialized nations such as the United States, the average daily water consumption is generally between _____ gallons per capita per day.

    A. 14 to 65
    B. 67 to 140
    C. 92 to 225
    D. 136 to 360

    5.____

6. Which of the following is NOT a by-product of ozonation?

    A. Epoxides
    B. Trihalomethanes (THMs)
    C. Unsaturated aldehydes
    D. Organic peroxides

    6.____

7. Which of the following compounds has the lowest maximum contaminant level(MCL, in mg/L) assigned by the EPA?

   A. Chlordane
   B. Styrene
   C. Carbon tetrachloride .005
   D. Toluene

8. Which of the following is NOT approved as a heterotrophic plate count method?

   A. Spread plate
   B. Membrane filter
   C. multiple-tube fermentation
   D. Pour plate

9. Under the Safe Drinking Water Act, the standard for acceptable color in drinking water is _____ total color units (TCU).

   A. 5
   B. 15
   C. 30
   D. 50

10. Conventional ion exchange units operate about the same as

    A. sludge scrapers
    B. solids-contact units
    C. flocculation basins
    D. downflow granular filters

11. The expected surface loading rate (SLR) during activated carbon treatment is usually _____ gpm/sq.ft.

    A. 2-5
    B. 5-12
    C. 10-15
    D. 12-22

12. Which of the following is NOT considered to be a reliable method for determining fluorine ion concentration?

    A. Dithizone method
    B. Complexone method
    C. Ion selective electrode method
    D. Colorimetric method

13. Which of the following is generally insoluble once oxidized in a solution with a pH of 7-8.5?

    A. Sodium
    B. Iron
    C. Chlorine
    D. Manganese

14. Which of the following chlorine compounds is NOT typically applied for the purpose of disinfection? 14.____

    A. Chlorine dioxide
    B. Chlorine gas
    C. Chlorite
    D. Hypochlorite

15. Which of the following inorganic chemicals is NOT carginogenic? 15.____

    A. Chromium
    B. Selenium
    C. Fluoride
    D. Cadmium

16. Monitoring for man-made radionuclides is required for surface water systems serving _____ persons or more. 16.____

    A. 10,000
    B. 40,000
    C. 100,000
    D. 400,000

17. Large-sized filter beds in treatment plants are generally limited to between _____ mc/day. 17.____

    A. 1,000-5,000
    B. 1,000-14,000
    C. 2,000-40,000
    D. 3,000-60,000

18. What is considered to be the reasonable range (mg/L) of sodium content in a water supply? 18.____

    A. 0.05-0.20
    B. 0.1-0.2
    C. 5-15
    D. 20-200

19. Which of the following coagulants is most effective when the water to be treated is not sufficiently alkaline? 19.____

    A. Activated silica
    B. Soda ash
    C. Liquid alum
    D. Ferric chloride

20. According to the federal Criteria for Evaluation and Standards Specifications, which of the following is classified as a Type C inorganic chemical? 20.____

    A. Lead
    B. Potassium
    C. Cyanide
    D. Zinc

21. The volumetric method, according to Standard Methods, is an acceptable analysis for detecting the presence of

   A. acidic herbicides
   B. methane
   C. PCBs
   D. phenols

22. Any tap in a system used as a sampling point should be without attachment, and should run for a minimum of _____ or more.

   A. 10 seconds
   B. 30 seconds
   C. 2 minutes
   D. 10 minutes

23. Aromatic compounds generally include

   A. esters
   B. halides
   C. ketones
   D. ethers

24. During coagulation, operational limits generally require that alum dosage be maintained between _____ ppm.

   A. 5-10
   B. 10-50
   C. 50-100
   D. 100-200

25. "Plain sedimentation" occurs when

   A. coagulation is eliminated
   B. disinfection is eliminated
   C. filtration is eliminated
   D. there is no in take-to-output flow

KEY (CORRECT ANSWERS)

1. D
2. B
3. B
4. C
5. C

6. B
7. C
8. B
9. B
10. D

11. A
12. A
13. B
14. C
15. C

16. C
17. C
18. D
19. B
20. B

21. B
22. C
23. C
24. B
25. A

EXAMINATION SECTION
TEST 1

DIRECTIONS: Each question or incomplete statement is followed by several suggested answers or completions. Select the one that BEST answers the question or completes the statement. *PRINT THE LETTER OF THE CORRECT ANSWER IN THE SPACE AT THE RIGHT.*

1. Photosynthesis is a process whereby a plant 1.____
   - A. gives off oxygen
   - B. takes in carbon dioxide
   - C. makes food
   - D. makes starch

2. _____ does NOT make its own food. 2.____
   - A. Mushroom
   - B. Geranium
   - C. African violet
   - D. Corn

3. The key chemical necessary for plants to make their own food is 3.____
   - A. oxygen
   - B. chlorophyll
   - C. carbon dioxide
   - D. starch

4. One substance spreading EVENLY through another is called 4.____
   - A. mixing   B. combining   C. diffusion   D. blending

5. The outer covering on the leaf of a plant is called 5.____
   - A. stomates
   - B. chloroplasts
   - C. guard cell
   - D. epidermis

6. The BEST soil for growing a garden is 6.____
   - A. sand   B. clay   C. loam   D. humus

7. When distilled water is thoroughly mixed with soil and the water filtered off and heated until all the water has been evaporated, a whitish material will be found in the evaporating dish. 7.____
   This is an example of
   - A. carbon dioxide in water
   - B. soil residue left in water
   - C. soil water having dissolved minerals in it
   - D. a poor filter

8. Asexual reproduction involves _____ parent(s). 8.____
   - A. no
   - B. two
   - C. one
   - D. two or more

9. _____ is NOT a structure of a flower. 9.____
   - A. Pollen   B. Stamen   C. Pistol   D. Ovary

10. One of the following pairs is MOST necessary for fertilization in a flower to take place:

    A. petals and limbs
    B. stamens and pistols
    C. ovules and ovary
    D. none of the above

11. A scientist cuts the tails off of two parent rats. Their offspring will

    A. have no tails
    B. have shorter tails
    C. some will have tails; others will not
    D. have normal tails

12. The BEST example of an acquired trait would be

    A. a rat with its tail cut off
    B. long legs
    C. a long nose
    D. a white crow

13. An early scientist who experimented to find out what traits in peas could be inherited was

    A. Helmont   B. Pasteur   C. Frosch   D. Mendel

14. Two pink flowers are mated. Of the four offspring, one is red, two are pink, and one is white.
    This is the result of a

    A. dominant trait
    B. hybrid
    C. recessive trait
    D. dominant and recessive trait

15. An inherited trait in offspring is decided by the

    A. parents
    B. sperm cell
    C. genes
    D. ovary

16. An archer who releases an arrow from a drawn bow provides an example of _____ energy.

    A. radiant
    B. mechanical
    C. chemical
    D. heat

17. A can of gasoline is BEST described as an example of _____ energy.

    A. kinetic
    B. mechanical
    C. heat
    D. potential

18. All energy that is of practical use in our world comes from _____ energy.

    A. radiant
    B. mechanical
    C. chemical
    D. heat

19. Striking a match so that it bursts into flame is an example of _____ energy.

    A. heat
    B. potential
    C. transformed
    D. kinetic

20. What gas in the atmosphere is ESSENTIAL for burning? 20.____

    A. Oxygen B. Nitrogen
    C. Water vapor D. Carbon dioxide

21. Chemicals A and B are to be mixed in a ratio of 3 to 4. If 12 grams of Chemical B are used, how many grams of Chemical A will be needed? 21.____

    A. 6 B. 8 C. 9 D. 16

22. A meter is a unit of length CLOSEST to a(n) 22.____

    A. inch B. foot C. yard D. mile

23. _____ does NOT affect the length of time it takes a planet to revolve around the sun. 23.____

    A. Size of planet
    B. Length of orbit
    C. Distance from sun
    D. Gravitational pull of sun

24. The volume of a box that is 3 cm long, 3 cm wide, and 2 cm high is _____ cm^3. 24.____

    A. 8 B. 9 C. 11 D. 18

25. An instrument used to record movements in the earth's crust is a 25.____

    A. barograph B. seismograph
    C. thermograph D. spectrograph

KEY (CORRECT ANSWERS)

1.	C	11.	D
2.	A	12.	A
3.	B	13.	D
4.	C	14.	B
5.	D	15.	C
6.	C	16.	B
7.	C	17.	D
8.	C	18.	A
9.	A	19.	C
10.	B	20.	A

21. C
22. C
23. A
24. D
25. B

TEST 2

DIRECTIONS: Each question or incomplete statement is followed by several suggested answers or completions. Select the one that BEST answers the question or completes the statement. *PRINT THE LETTER OF THE CORRECT ANSWER IN THE SPACE AT THE RIGHT.*

1. Work is done when

   A. you exert a force upon an object
   B. you expend energy
   C. a force moves an object
   D. all of the above

   1.___

2. Work is measured by the

   A. amount of force exerted to move an object
   B. amount of energy used to move an object
   C. distance an object is moved
   D. amount of force multiplied by the distance an object is moved

   2.___

3. A boy's car runs out of gas. He struggles to push it to a gas station. He is attempting to overcome

   A. gravity   B. resistance   C. friction   D. inertia

   3.___

4. John had a flat tire, but had no jack. He used a fence post and a large rock to raise the car.
   This illustrates

   A. the lever
   C. John's strength
   B. the fulcrum
   D. the auto's resistance

   4.___

5. Energy can be BEST explained as the

   A. capacity to do work
   B. amount of work done
   C. amount of force expended
   D. amount of force times the distance an object is moved

   5.___

6. One of the oldest and simplest machines is the

   A. crow bar
   C. pulley
   B. inclined plane
   D. steam engine

   6.___

7. The useful work one gets from a machine is _____ the work put in.

   A. always less than
   C. always greater than
   B. always equal to
   D. sometimes greater than

   7.___

8. Efficiency is measured by

   A. the amount of useful work obtained from a machine
   B. the amount of work put in a machine
   C. A times B
   D. A divided by B

   8.___

36

9. A block and tackle can be used to lift extremely heavy weight because it   9._____

   A. is fixed
   B. is movable
   C. has a large mechanical advantage
   D. has no friction

10. Inertia is BEST described as   10._____

    A. the tendency of an object to remain at rest
    B. the tendency of an object in motion to keep on going
    C. both of the above
    D. none of the above

11. Very rapid burning of fuel is BEST described as   11._____

    A. spontaneous combustion   B. an explosion
    C. ignition   D. work

12. A gasoline engine produces a dangerous gas called   12._____

    A. nitrogen   B. carbon monoxide
    C. carbon dioxide   D. carbon-nitrate

13. The man who invented the diesel engine was   13._____

    A. Rudolf Diesel   B. James Watt
    C. Charles Parsons   D. Thomas Savery

14. Static electricity is caused by   14._____

    A. a dynamo   B. a mechanical generator
    C. friction   D. electrons

15. An atom has   15._____

    A. the same number of electrons and protons
    B. more electrons than protons
    C. more protons than electrons
    D. a number of protons and electrons equal to one-half the number of neutrons

16. A gasoline truck drags a chain on the ground in order to   16._____

    A. discharge neutrons   B. discharge electrons
    C. discharge protons   D. take on protons

17. Another name for a battery is   17._____

    A. voltmeter   B. amperstand
    C. Gilberts box   D. Voltaic pile

18. An electric current can BEST be described as   18._____

    A. protons moving to neutrons   B. a flow of protons
    C. a flow of neutrons   D. a flow of electrons

19. A TRUE statement about magnets is:

    A. Magnets attract iron
    B. One end of a bar magnet will point north
    C. Like poles of magnets repel each other
    D. All of the above

20. Soil is DIFFERENT from rock because soil

    A. is dark in color
    B. supports plant life
    C. is heavier than rock
    D. does not contain minerals

21. The LARGEST river drainage system in the United States is the _____ River and its tributaries.

    A. Hudson
    B. Amazon
    C. Columbia
    D. Mississippi

22. All invertebrate animals lack

    A. a brain
    B. a backbone
    C. arms or legs
    D. sensory organs

23. _____ is the HARDEST substance.

    A. Calcite
    B. Quartz
    C. Copper
    D. Graphite

24. _____ CANNOT be classified as a fossil.

    A. A shell of a clam washed ashore on a beach
    B. A grasshopper preserved in volcanic ash
    C. The impression of a fern leaf in a piece of coal
    D. The footprint of a dinosaur found in a solid rock

25. An object that orbits a planet is called a(n)

    A. star
    B. meteorite
    C. satellite
    D. asteroid

KEY (CORRECT ANSWERS)

1. C
2. D
3. B
4. A
5. A

6. B
7. A
8. D
9. C
10. C

11. B
12. B
13. A
14. C
15. A

16. B
17. D
18. D
19. D
20. B

21. D
22. B
23. B
24. A
25. C

TEST 3

DIRECTIONS: Each question or incomplete statement is followed by several suggested answers or completions. Select the one that BEST answers the question or completes the statement. *PRINT THE LETTER OF THE CORRECT ANSWER IN THE SPACE AT THE RIGHT.*

1. According to the metric system, the _____ is a unit of measure for weight. 1.____
   A. meter B. pound C. kilogram D. liter

2. A germ killer made by a living organism is called a(n) 2.____
   A. toxin B. antitoxin C. anopheles D. antibiotic

3. The position of a satellite at a point in its orbit when it is FURTHEST away from the earth is called its 3.____
   A. altitude B. apogee C. perigee D. attitude

4. Men in outer space need LEAST worry about 4.____
   A. oxygen B. radiation C. gravity D. meteors

5. When traveling from Philadelphia to San Francisco, one's watch should be set _____ hours. 5.____
   A. back three B. ahead four
   C. ahead three D. back four

6. The amount of water vapor present in air is called 6.____
   A. precipitation B. BTU
   C. humidity D. evaporation

7. A surface which reflects NEARLY all visible wave lengths appears as 7.____
   A. black B. white C. red D. violet

8. The surface of the earth is covered by _____% of land. 8.____
   A. 70 B. 75 C. 65 D. 30

9. An element NOT known until made by scientists is 9.____
   A. uranium B. radium C. helium D. plutonium

10. Cement is made by mixing clay and 10.____
    A. concrete B. gravel C. limestone D. sand

11. Soft coal, heated in a test tube, does NOT produce 11.____
    A. coal tar B. charcoal C. coke D. gas

12. Of the following traits, _____ are inherited. 12.____
    A. likes and dislikes B. opinions
    C. eye color D. handwriting

13. Nitrogen can BEST be added to the soil by planting 13.____

    A. clover   B. corn   C. potatoes   D. wheat

14. The dinosaur provides an example of lack of 14.____

    A. balance   B. adaptation
    C. fertilization   D. maneuverability

15. Because herons were thought to be destroying fishing grounds, a bounty was offered for every heron killed. After most of the herons were killed, fishing improved for a while, but then began to decrease. 15.____
    This is an example of the need for

    A. balance   B. adaptation
    C. better food supply   D. fewer fishermen

16. One can describe lightning as being 16.____

    A. the result of thunder
    B. usually harmful
    C. a kind of electric spark
    D. a vacuum

17. If three 1 1/2 volt dry cell batteries are connected in series and measured by a voltmeter, the reading would be _____ volts. 17.____

    A. 1 1/2   B. 3   C. 3 1/2   D. 4 1/2

18. Newton's third law of motion is BEST illustrated by a(n) 18.____

    A. apple falling from a tree
    B. rocket taking off
    C. can of gasoline
    D. radio transmitter

19. In a gasoline engine, combustion is caused by 19.____

    A. compression
    B. gasoline
    C. a mixture of air and gasoline
    D. a spark plug

20. A light-year is a measure of 20.____

    A. time   B. speed   C. distance   D. brightness

21. The classification of rocks into three major groups is PRIMARILY based upon differences in 21.____

    A. age   B. size   C. origin   D. hardness

22. Isobars on a weather map connect points of equal 22.____

    A. temperature   B. air pressure
    C. precipitation   D. wind direction

23. The negatively-charged particle within an atom is called a(n)   23.___
    A. photon   B. proton   C. neutron   D. electron

24. In the ocean, MOST surface waves are a result of   24.___
    A. tides   B. wind action
    C. earthquakes   D. the revolution of the earth

25. Which of these is a unit of volume?   25.___
    A. Ton   B. Gram   C. Liter   D. Kilometer

KEY (CORRECT ANSWERS)

1. C   11. B
2. D   12. C
3. B   13. A
4. C   14. B
5. A   15. A

6. C   16. C
7. B   17. D
8. D   18. B
9. D   19. D
10. C   20. C

21. C
22. B
23. D
24. B
25. C

EXAMINATION SECTION
TEST 1

DIRECTIONS: Each question or incomplete statement is followed by several suggested answers or completions. Select the one that BEST answers the question or completes the statement. PRINT THE LETTER OF THE CORRECT ANSWER IN THE SPACE AT THE RIGHT.

1. 65° centigrade is equivalent to _____ F. 1.____

    A. 85° B. 97° C. 117° D. 149° E. 338°

2. 65° centigrade is equivalent to _____ absolute. 2.____

    A. 85° B. 97° C. 117° D. 149° E. 338°

3. The formula $CuSO_4 \cdot 5H_2O$ represents a compound containing 3.____

    A. carbon
    B. 4 different elements
    C. 5 different elements
    D. 11 different atoms
    E. 12 different atoms

4. Sodium sulfate would be classified as a(n) 4.____

    A. element B. compound C. mixture
    D. acid E. base

5. An element in the *same* family of the periodic table as sodium that would be predicted to be *more* active than sodium is 5.____

    A. Rb B. Cl C. C D. Ca
    E. none of these

6. The predicted formula of the compound of calcium and chlorine is 6.____

    A. Ca_2Cl B. $CaCl$ C. $CaCl_2$ D. $CaCl_3$ E. $CaCl_4$

7. The predicted formula of the compound of phosphorus and hydrogen would be 7.____

    A. HP B. H_2P C. PH_3 D. PH_4 E. PH_5

8. The predicted formula for the compound of nitrogen and oxygen would be 8.____

    A. N_2O B. NO C. NO_2 D. N_2O_4 E. N_2O_5

9. Hydrogen may be prepared by reacting an acid with a(n) 9.____

    A. metal oxide B. acid anhydride C. active metal
    D. metal sulfate E. all of these

10. Hydrogen chloride reacts with water to form 10.____

    A. H_3O^+ and OH^- B. H_3O^+ and Cl^- C. H_2O and Cl^-
    D. H_2O and HCl E. OH^- and HCl

43

11. The MOST active nonmetal is

    A. chlorine   B. oxygen   C. fluorine
    D. sulfur   E. sodium

12. A water solution of _____ would turn blue litmus pink.

    A. NH_3 B. MgO   C. CaO   D. SO_2 E. LiH

13. The reaction of a soluble metallic oxide with water produces a(n)

    A. salt   B. base   C. acid
    D. anhydride   E. alcohol

14. A good example of a chemical change is the

    A. boiling of water
    B. souring of milk
    C. grinding of corn
    D. dissolving of sodium chloride in water
    E. distillation of ethyl alcohol

15. The MOST abundant element is

    A. iron   B. aluminum   C. sodium
    D. nitrogen   E. oxygen

16. An example of an element that would be classified as a nonmetal is

    A. phosphorus   B. gold   C. calcium
    D. bismuth   E. helium

17. The symbol, Co, represents

    A. carbon   B. carbon monoxide   C. cobalt
    D. cobalt oxide   E. copper

18. A good example of a mixture is

    A. potassium chlorate   B. carbon dioxide
    C. oxygen gas   D. milk
    E. cane sugar, $C_{12}H_{22}O_{11}$

19. A compound containing *only* zinc and sulfur would be named zinc

    A. sulfate   B. sulfite   C. sulfide
    D. disulfate   E. disulfide

20. The formula $C_{17}H_{35}COONa$ represents a compound containing

    A. nitrogen   B. 35 atoms of hydrogen
    C. 17 atoms of carbon   D. 35 atoms of carbon
    E. 6 different elements

21. A compound containing 50% sulfur, atomic weight 32, and 50% oxygen, atomic weight 16, could have the formula

    A. S_2O B. SO   C. S_2O_3 D. SO_2 E. SO_3

22. The CORRECT formula followed by the CORRECT name is   22._____
    A. H_3PO_4, phosphorus acid   B. HNO_3, nitrous acid
    C. H_2SO_3, sulfurous acid   D. $HClO_4$, chloric acid
    E. HNO_2, nitric acid

23. A two molar solution of sulfuric acid, molecular weight 98, contains _____ grams solute   23._____
    per _____.
    A. 2; liter   B. 49; liter   C. 98; liter
    D. 196; liter   E. 392; 1000 grams water

24. Which liquid is considered a good conductor of electric current?   24._____
    A. Glacial acetic acid   B. Water
    C. Ethyl alcohol   D. Carbon tetrachloride
    E. A water solution of calcium chloride

25. _____ will exist as ions in water solutions.   25._____
    A. Sugar   B. Ethyl clcohol
    C. Carbon tetrachloride   D. Calcium chloride
    E. Glycerine

KEY (CORRECT ANSWERS)

1. D   11. C
2. E   12. D
3. B   13. B
4. B   14. B
5. A   15. E

6. C   16. A
7. C   17. C
8. E   18. D
9. C   19. C
10. B   20. B

21. D
22. C
23. D
24. E
25. D

TEST 2

DIRECTIONS: Each question or incompelte statement is followed by several suggested answers or completions. Select the one that *BEST* answers the question or completes the statement. *PRINT THE LETTER OF THE CORRECT ANSWER IN THE SPACE AT THE RIGHT.*

1. Sodium chloride would be classified as a(n)   1.___
   - A. element
   - B. compound
   - C. mixture
   - D. acid
   - E. base

2. An element in the same family as bromine and more electronegative than bromine is   2.___
   - A. iodine
   - B. sodium
   - C. oxygen
   - D. chlorine
   - E. carbon

3. The predicted formula of the compound of phosphorus and oxygen is   3.___
   - A. P_2O_3
   - B. PO_3
   - C. P_2O_5
   - D. PO_4
   - E. P_2O_7

4. The predicted formula of the hydrogen and sulfur compound is   4.___
   - A. HS_2
   - B. HS
   - C. H_2S
   - D. H_3S
   - E. H_6S

5. Which substance produces the GREATEST lowering of the freezing point when a molecular or formula weight of the substance is dissolved in 1000 grams of water?   5.___
   - A. $C_{12}H_{22}O_{11}$
   - B. $C_2H_6O_2$
   - C. $CaCl_2$
   - D. $NaCl$
   - E. CH_3OH

6. _____ acid is *highly* ionized in water and is *also* a strong oxidizing agent.   6.___
   - A. Acetic
   - B. Nitric
   - C. Phosphoric
   - D. Citric
   - E. Hydrochloric

7. Water has a *higher* boiling point than hydrogen sulfide because   7.___
   - A. ionization is incomplete
   - B. there is a small amount of deuterium in water
   - C. water molecules form large aggregates due to hydrogen bonding
   - D. hydrogen sulfide has the larger molecular weight
   - E. hydrogen sulfide ionizes to a slight extent

8. The class of impurities removed from water by typical distillation procedures is _____ ones.   8.___
   - A. volatile
   - B. all soluble
   - C. nonvolatile
   - D. all condensable
   - E. all acidic

9. A normal solution is defined as a solution containing one gram   9.___
   - A. molecular weight of solute per liter of solution
   - B. molecular weight of solute per thousand grams of solvent
   - C. solute per thousand grams solvent
   - D. equivalent weight of solute per liter of solution
   - E. equivalent weight of solute per thousand grams of solvent

10. Water is a good solvent for

    A. CH_3OH B. CH_4 C. CS_2 D. C_8H_{18} E. CCl_4

11. One oxygen atom weighs (the atomic weight of oxygen is 16 and Avogadros number is 6.02×10^{23})

    A. 16 grams
    B. 16 atomic weight units
    C. 6.02×10^{23} atomic weight units
    D. 6.02×10^{23} grams
    E. 1 gram

12. One gram of sulfur (atomic weight 32) contains

    A. one thirty-second atom of sulfur
    B. 32 atoms sulfur
    C. 1.9×10^{22} atoms of sulfur
    D. 6.02×10^{23} atoms of sulfur
    E. 1 mole of sulfur

13. One mole of H_3PO_4 contains

    A. 1 gram of hydrogen
    B. 16 grams of oxygen
    C. 93 grams phosphorus
    D. 3 moles of atoms
    E. 8 moles of atoms

14. One molecule of gas A reacts with three molecules of gas B to produce two molecules of gas C and no other substance. Gas A contains

    A. 1 atom   B. 2 atoms   C. 3 atoms
    D. 5 atoms   E. all of the above

15. Potassium chlorate ($KClO_3$) will decompose to give oxygen gas and potassium chloride. One sixth mole potassium chlorate will yield

    A. one sixth mole oxygen   B. 1 gram oxygen
    C. 8 grams oxygen   D. 16 grams oxygen
    E. 22.4 liters of oxygen

16. Sodium metal (Na) reacts with chlorine gas (Cl_2) to form salt (NaCl). One gram of sodium would react with

    A. 1 gram of chlorine
    B. 1/23 mole chlorine
    C. approximately .5 liters of chlorine at STP
    D. 71 grams of chlorine
    E. approximately 1.0 liters of chlorine at STP

17. A flask contained .064 gram of oxygen gas. The same flask was filled with an unknown gas at the same temperature and pressure. This gas weighted .128 gram. The molecular weight of the unknown gas was

   A. 8   B. 12.8   C. 16   D. 32   E. 64

18. Two grams of a gas occupies 2.24 liters at a temperature of 0° C. and a pressure of 760 mm of Hg.
The molecular weight of the gas is

   A. 2   B. 22.4   C. 20   D. 44.8   E. .89

19. Which one of the following gases would be predicted to exhibit the FASTEST rate of diffusion?

   A. NH_3 B. HCl   C. H_2 D. SO_2 E. CO_2

20. The position of an element in the periodic table is determined by

   A. electron configuration
   B. atomic mass
   C. atomic volume
   D. electronegativity
   E. period discovered

21. The concentration of which component of the atmosphere varies MOST?

   A. Oxygen
   B. Nitrogen
   C. Argon
   D. Water
   E. These all have fixed concentrations in the atmosphere

22. The MOST active nonmetal is

   A. chlorine
   B. oxygen
   C. sulfur
   D. sodium
   E. fluorine

23. In sodium chloride the bond between sodium and chlorine is classified as a(n)

   A. ionic bond
   B. covalent bond
   C. ion dipole bond
   D. metallic bond
   E. hydrogen bond

24. Acetic acid is classed as a weak acid because acetic acid

   A. is but slightly soluble in water
   B. is an organic acid
   C. gives a high concentration of acetate ions in solution
   D. reacts rapidly with zinc
   E. does NOT give high concentrations of hydronium ion in water solution

25. Hot concentrated sulfuric acid reacts with copper

   A. to form cupric sulfate and hydrogen
   B. because sulfuric acid behaves as an acid
   C. because hot concentrated sulfuric acid is an oxidizing agent
   D. because copper is a metal
   E. because sulfuric acid is nonvolatile

KEY (CORRECT ANSWERS)

1. B
2. D
3. C
4. C
5. C

6. B
7. C
8. C
9. D
10. A

11. B
12. C
13. E
14. B
15. C

16. C
17. E
18. C
19. C
20. A

21. D
22. E
23. A
24. E
25. C

TEST 3

DIRECTIONS: Each question or incomplete statement is followed by several suggested answers or completions. Select the one that *BEST* answers the question or completes the statement. *PRINT THE LETTER OF THE CORRECT ANSWER IN THE SPACE AT THE RIGHT.*

1. Aqueous solutions of acid

   A. turn red litmus blue
   B. react with copper to liberate hydrogen
   C. conduct an electric current
   D. are strong proton acceptors
   E. are characterized by the presence of hydroxide ions

   1.___

2. An example of a weak acid is

   A. hydrochloric acid
   B. nitric acid
   C. sulfuric acid
   D. acetic acid
   E. ammonium hydroxide

   2.___

3. Hydrogen sulfide (a weak acid of formula H_2S) reacts with water to form *mainly*

   A. $H_3O^+ + S^=$
   B. $H^+ + S^=$
   C. $H_3O^+ + HS^-$
   D. $2H_3O^+ + S^=$
   E. $H_3S+ + OH-$

   3.___

4. In pure water at 25°C, the concentration of hydronium ion (hydrogen ion) is _____ moles/liter.

   A. 10^{-14} B. 10^{-7} C. 10^{-5} D. 1   E. 7

   4.___

5. A container suitable for storage of aqueous solutions of $Fe_2(SO_4)_3$ could be made of

   A. nickle   B. zinc   C. tin
   D. lead   E. silver

   5.___

6. With what volume of .600 normal NaOH would 100 ml of .150 normal H_2SO_4 react? _____

   A. 25.0   B. 50.0   C. 100   D. 200   E. 400

   6.___

7. Vegetable oils are often hydrogenated to

   A. prevent their hydrolysis
   B. decrease their melting point
   C. make them solids at room temperature
   D. prepare soap
   E. make them dry faster

   7.___

8. The weight of one liter of hydrogen at STP is _____ gram(s).

   A. .089   B. .045   C. 1.0   D. 2.0   E. 89.0

   8.___

50

9. The numerical value of the vapor pressure of ether at its boiling point is _____ mm of Hg.

   A. 22.4   B. 100   C. 224   D. 760   E. 1000

9.____

10. If ten grams of ice at 0°C is melted and converted to liquid water at 20°C it requires _____ calories.

    A. 20   B. 80   C. 200   D. 800   E. 1000

10.____

11. The products formed when sulfuric acid reacts with water are _____ ion and _____ ion.

    A. hydronium; sulfate
    B. hydronium; sulfide
    C. hydronium; sulfite
    D. hydronium; hydroxide
    E. hydrogen; sulfide

11.____

12. A salt solution is boiling.
    As the water boils away the temperature

    A. is 100 degrees
    B. remains constant
    C. decreases
    D. increases
    E. depends on the source of heat

12.____

13. Two clear liquids, when mixed with each other, yield a solid and a liquid.
    This represents

    A. precipitation   B. condensation   C. evaporation
    D. homogenization   E. sublimation

13.____

14. A strongly acid solution may have a pH of

    A. 0   B. 6   C. 7   D. 8   E. 14

14.____

15. In the elctrolysis of a concentrated sodium chloride solution, the substance produced at the positive electrode is

    A. sodium
    B. sodium hydroxide
    C. chlorine
    D. hydrogen
    E. sodium chloride

15.____

16. Silicon, which is in the same family as carbon, would be predicted to exhibit a valence of

    A. 1   B. 2   C. 3   D. 4   E. 5

16.____

17. The type of chemical bond that is considered to account for the *unusual* properties of water is a(n) _____ bond.

    A. ionic
    B. covalent
    C. hydrogen
    D. coordinate covalent
    E. ion dipole

17.____

18. Silver chloride will dissolve in ammonia solution because

    A. ammonia is a base
    B. the silver ammonia complex ion is formed
    C. of the common ion effect
    D. chlorine is an active nonmetal
    E. double decomposition reaction can occur

18.____

19. The following compound, CH_3COCH_3, would be classified as a(n)

    A. hydrocarbon   B. ether   C. ester
    D. aldehyde   E. ketone

20. The following compound, CH_3CH_2OH, would be classified as a(n)

    A. hydrocarbon   B. ester   C. alcohol
    D. aldehyde   E. ketone

21. A one tenth molar solution of hydrochloric acid would exhibit a pH of

    A. 1   B. 5   C. 7   D. 9   E. 13

22. A one tenth molar solution of sodium chloride would exhibit a pH of *approximately*

    A. 1   B. 5   C. 7   D. 9   E. 13

23. A one tenth molar solution of sodium hydroxide would exhibit a pH of *approximately*

    A. 1   B. 5   C. 7   D. 9   E. 13

24. The ion other than hydronium ion in LARGEST concentration in a 1 molar solution of phosphoric acid is

    A. PO_4^{-3} B. $H_2PO_4^-$ C. HPO_4^{-2}
    D. OH^- E. PO_3^{-3}

25. The class of compound to which $CH_3CH_2CH_2CH_3$ belongs is

    A. hydrocarbon   B. ether   C. ester
    D. aldehyde   E. ketone

KEY (CORRECT ANSWERS)

1. C
2. D
3. C
4. B
5. E

6. A
7. C
8. A
9. D
10. E

11. A
12. D
13. A
14. A
15. C

16. D
17. C
18. B
19. E
20. C

21. A
22. C
23. E
24. B
25. A

TEST 4

DIRECTIONS: Each question or incomplete statement is followed by several suggested answers or completions. Select the one that *BEST* answers the question or completes the statement. *PRINT THE LETTER OF THE CORRECT ANSWER IN THE SPACE AT THE RIGHT.*

1. When $CaCO_3$ is heated,

   A. oxygen is evolved
   B. calcium carbide is formed
   C. carbon monoxide is evolved
   D. carbon dioxide is evolved
   E. no chemical reaction occurs

1._____

Questions 2 - 6.

DIRECTIONS: Use the following reaction to answer questions 2-6.

$$2H_3PO_4 + 3Zn \rightarrow Zn_3(PO_4)_2 + 3H_2$$

using the atomic weights H = 1, O = 16, P = 31, Zn = 65.4

2. The molecular weight of H_3PO_4, phosphoric acid, is

   A. 2   B. 48   C. 96   D. 98   E. 196

2._____

3. Three gram atoms of zinc will yield

   A. three moles hydrogen
   B. three grams hydrogen
   C. three liters hydrogen at STP
   D. six moles hydrogen
   E. six liters hydrogen at STP

3._____

4. 392 grams phosphoric acid will yield

   A. 2 grams hydrogen   B. 6 grams hydrogen
   C. 12 grams hydrogen   D. 6 liters hydrogen at STP
   E. 12 liters hydrogen at STP

4._____

5. One mole of phosphoric acid will yield

   A. 1/2 mole zinc phosphate
   B. 1 mole zinc phosphate
   C. 2 moles zinc phosphate
   D. 3 moles hydrogen
   E. 22.4 liters of hydrogen at STP

5._____

6. 196 grams phosphoric acid will yield_____ liter(s) hydrogen at STP

   A. 1   B. 3   C. 22.4   D. 33.6   E. 67.2

6._____

2 (#4)

Questions 7-10

DIRECTIONS: For the reaction $H_2 + Cl_2 \rightarrow 2HCl$ using the atomic weights H= 1 and Cl = 35.5

7. Four liters of hydrogen would react with _____ liters chlorine. 7.___
   A. 2   B. 4   C. 35.5   D. 89.6   E. 142

8. 11.2 liters hydrogen at STP would yield _____ grams HCl. 8.___
   A. 2   B. 18.25   C. 36.5   D. 438.5   E. none of the above

9. 35.5 grams of chlorine would yield _____ grams HCl. 9.___
   A. 2   B. 35.5   C. 36.5   D. 71   E. 73

10. Three moles of HCl weigh _____ grams 10.___
    A. 3   B. 6   C. 36.5   D. 109.5   E. 219

11. The weight of one liter of oxygen gas at STP is _____ grams. 11.___
    A. 1.00   B. .72   C. 1.42   D. 16.0   E. 32.0

12. The molecular weight of a gas that exhibits a density of 3.2 grams per liter at STP is 12.___
    A. 3.2   B. 22.4   C. 32   D. 71.5   E. 7.0

13. The *approximate* volume of 3 moles of chlorine gas (molecular weight 71) at STP is _____ liters. 13.___
    A. 3   B. 22.4   C. 67   D. 71   E. 213

14. The volume of a gas doubles at constant pressure. The temperature 14.___
    A. remains constant
    B. doubles in degrees absolute
    C. is decreased to 1/2 the original value in degrees absolute
    D. was 273 degrees absolute
    E. increases to 4 times the original value in degrees centigrade

15. The numerical value of the vapor pressure of water at 100° centigrade is _____ mm of Hg. 15.___
    A. 22.4   B. 100   C. 224   D. 760   E. 1000

16. If 100 grams of ice at 0° C is melted and converted to liquid water at 20° C it requires _____ calories. 16.___
    A. 20   B. 80   C. 2000   D. 8000   E. 10,000

17. 64 grams of methyl alcohol, formula weight 32, dissolved in 1000 grams of water would be predicted to exhibit a freezing point of 17.___
    A. −.93°C   B. −1.86°C   C. −3.72°C   D. 0°C   E. 1.86°C

18. The coefficient that would appear in front of NaOH when the following equation is balanced is

    NaOH + H_2SO_4 → Na_2SO_4 + H_2O

    A. 1   B. 2   C. 3   D. 4   E. 5

19. For the reaction $KClO_3$ → KCl + O_2, the coefficient that would appear in front of oxygen in the balanced equation is

    A. 1   B. 2   C. 3   D. 4   E. 5

20. For the reaction HgO → Hg + O_2, the coefficient that would appear in front of mercury in the balanced equation is

    A. 1   B. 2   C. 3   D. 4   E. 5

21. For the reaction Al + H_2SO_4 → $Al_2(SO_4)_3$ + H_2, the coefficient that would appear in front of hydrogen in the balanced equation is

    A. 1   B. 2   C. 3   D. 4   E. 5

22. For the reaction Mg + O_2 → MgO, the coefficient that would appear in front of magnesium oxide in the balanced equation would be

    A. 1   B. 2   C. 3   D. 4   E. 5

23. For the reaction SO_2 + O_2 → SO_3, the coefficient that would appear in front of SO_2 in the balanced equation is

    A. 1   B. 2   C. 3   D. 4   E. 5

24. For the reaction ZnS + O_2 → ZnO + SO_2, the coefficient that would appear in front of oxygen in the balanced equation is

    A. 1   B. 2   C. 3   D. 4   E. 5

25. For the reaction C_2H_5OH + O_2 → CO_2 + H_2O the coefficient that would appear in front of oxygen in the balanced equation is

    A. 2   B. 3   C. 4   D. 7   E. none of these

KEY (CORRECT ANSWERS)

1. D
2. D
3. A
4. C
5. A

6. E
7. B
8. C
9. E
10. D

11. C
12. D
13. C
14. B
15. D

16. E
17. C
18. B
19. C
20. B

21. C
22. B
23. B
24. C
25. B

EXAMINATION SECTION
TEST 1

DIRECTIONS: Each question or incomplete statement is followed by several suggested answers or completions. Select the one that BEST answers the question or completes the statement. *PRINT THE LETTER OF THE CORRECT ANSWER IN THE SPACE AT THE RIGHT.*

Questions 1-17.

DIRECTIONS: Questions 1 through 17 are to be answered on the basis of the tools shown below and on the following page. The numbers in the answers refer to the numbers beneath the tools.

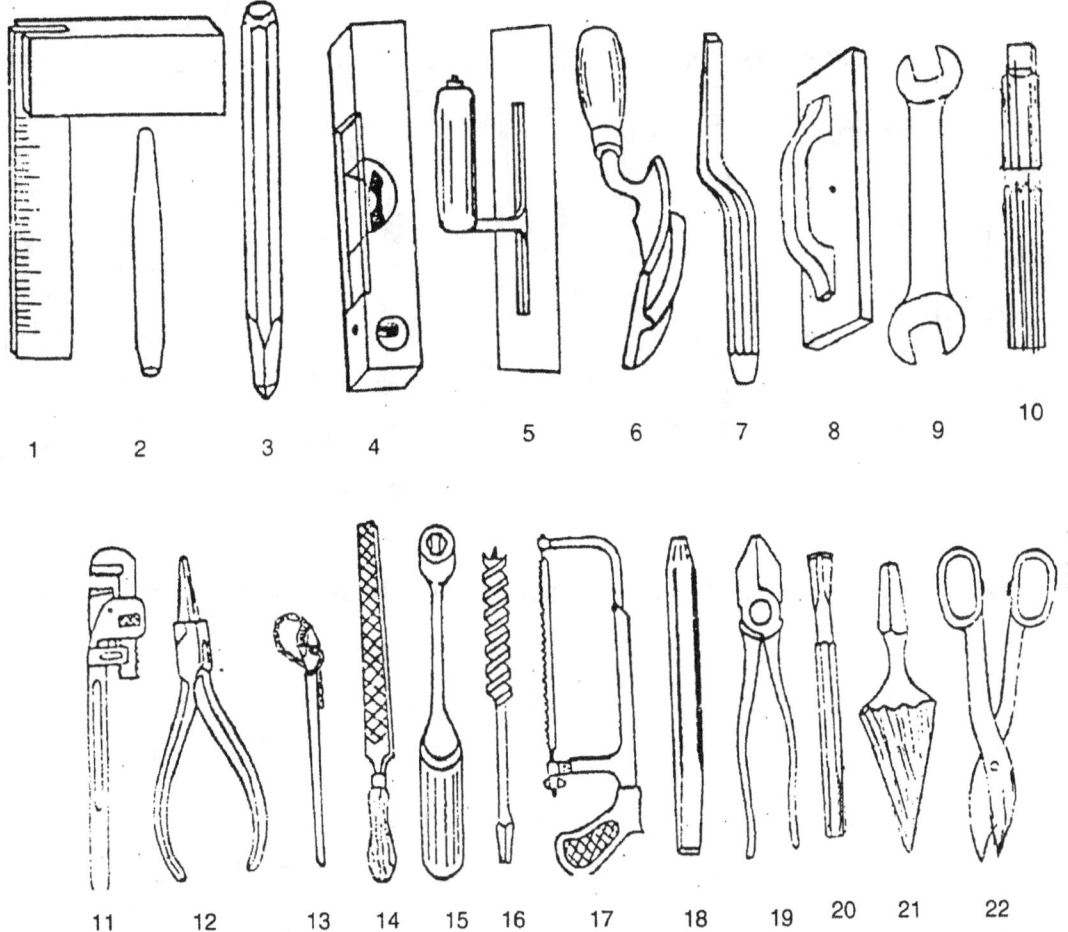

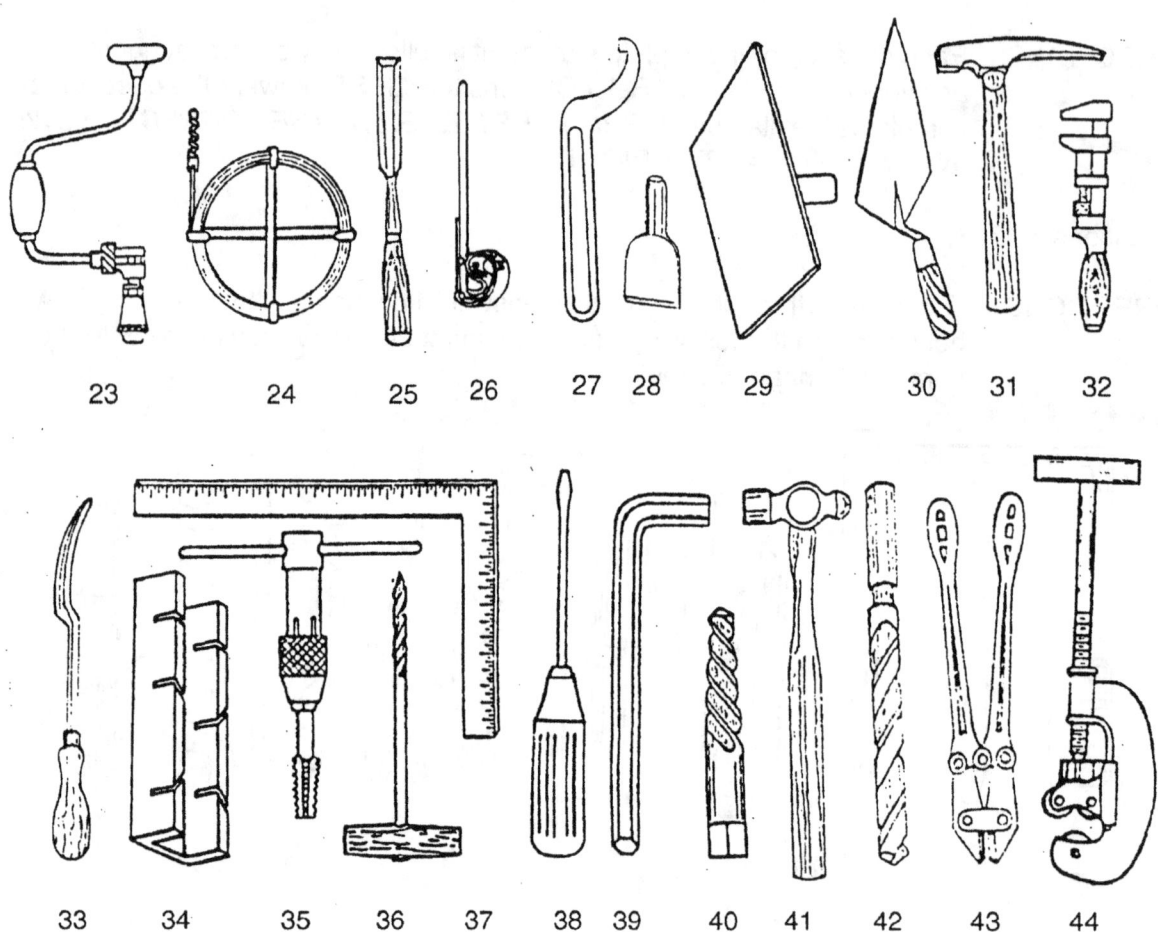

1. To tighten an elbow onto a threaded pipe, a mechanic should use tool number
   A. 9   B. 11   C. 26   D. 32

2. To cut grooves in newly poured cement, a mechanic should use tool number
   A. 5   B. 6   C. 28   D. 29

3. To *caulk* a lead joint, a mechanic should use tool number
   A. 7   B. 10   C. 25   D. 33

4. The term *snips* should be applied by a mechanic to tool number
   A. 12   B. 22   C. 36   D. 43

5. To slightly enlarge an existing 17/32" diameter hole in a metal plate, a mechanic should use tool number
   A. 3   B. 10   C. 14   D. 35

6. The term *snake* should be applied by a mechanic to tool number
   A. 21   B. 23   C. 24   D. 40

7. If the threaded portion of a 1/2" brass pipe breaks off inside a gate valve, the piece should be removed with tool number   7.____
   A. 15   B. 35   C. 39   D. 40

8. To cut a face brick into a bat, a mechanic should use tool number   8.____
   A. 3   B. 18   C. 25   D. 28

9. A mechanic should cut a 3" x 2" x 3/16" angle iron with tool number   9.____
   A. 3   B. 17   C. 22   D. 43

10. A mechanic should tighten a chrome-plated water supply pipe by using tool number   10.____
    A. 11   B. 19   C. 26   D. 32

11. The term *hawk* should be applied by a mechanic to tool number   11.____
    A. 28   B. 29   C. 30   D. 33

12. If your co-worker asks you to pass him the *star* drill, you should hand him tool number   12.____
    A. 16   B. 20   C. 40   D. 42

13. After threading a 1" diameter piece of pipe, a mechanic should debur the inside by using tool number   13.____
    A. 14   B. 21   C. 36   D. 40

14. A mechanic should apply the term *float* to tool number   14.____
    A. 4   B. 6   C. 8   D. 28

15. If a mechanic has to cut a dozen 15-inch lengths of 3/4-inch steel pipe for spacers, he should use tool number   15.____
    A. 18   B. 26   C. 43   D. 44

16. If a mechanic is erecting two structural steel plates and needs to line up the bolt holes, he should use tool number   16.____
    A. 2   B. 3   C. 33   D. 42

17. To cut reinforcing wire mesh to be used in a concrete floor, you should use tool number   17.____
    A. 7   B. 17   C. 18   D. 43

18. The MAIN reason for overhauling a power tool on a regular basis is to   18.____
    A. make the men more familiar with the tool
    B. keep the men busy during slack times
    C. insure that the tool is used occasionally
    D. minimize breakdowns

19. A mechanic should NOT press too heavily on a hacksaw while using it to cut through a steel rod because this may   19.____
    A. create flying steel particles   B. bend the frame
    C. break the blade   D. overheat the rod

20. Creosote is commonly used with wood to

   A. speed-up the seasoning
   B. make the wood fireproof
   C. make painting easier
   D. preserve the wood

21. A mitre box should be used to

   A. hold a saw while sharpening it
   B. store expensive tools
   C. hold a saw at a fixed angle
   D. encase steel beams for protection

22. Wood scaffold planks should be inspected

   A. at regular intervals
   B. before they are stored away
   C. once a week
   D. each time before they are used

23. Continuous sheeting should be used when excavating deep trenches in

   A. rock
   B. stiff clay
   C. firm earth
   D. unstable soil

24. The MAIN reason for requiring that certain special tools be returned to the tool room after a job has been completed is that

   A. missing tools can be replaced
   B. the men will not need to care for the tools
   C. more tools will be available for use
   D. this permits easier inspection and maintenance of tools

25. The BEST material to use to extinguish an oil fire is

   A. sand
   B. water
   C. sawdust
   D. stone gravel

26. A *lally* column is

   A. fabricated from angles and plates
   B. fabricated by tying two channels together with lattice bars
   C. a steel member that has unequal sections
   D. a pipe fitted with a base plate at each end

27. The BEST action for you to take if you discover a small puddle of oil on the shop floor is to FIRST

   A. have it cleaned up
   B. find out who spilled it
   C. discover the source of the leak
   D. cover it with newspaper

28. You should listen to your foreman even when he insists on explaining the procedure for a job you have done many times before because

    A. you can do the job the way you want when he leaves
    B. he may make an error and you can show that you know your job
    C. it is wise to humor him even if he is wrong
    D. you are required to do the job the way the foreman wants it

28.____

Questions 29-34.

DIRECTIONS: Questions 29 through 34 refer to the sketches shown to the right of each question.

29. The indicated pressure is MOST NEARLY _____ psi.
    A. 132
    B. 137
    C. 143
    D. 148

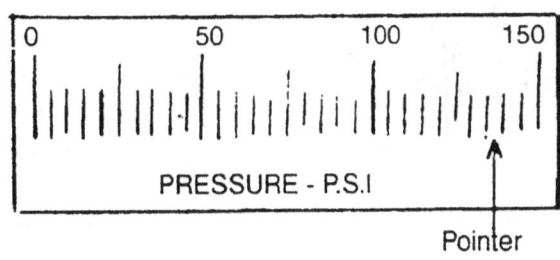

29.____

30. The fewest number of shims, of any combination of thicknesses, required to exactly fill the 1/4" gap shown is
    A. 7
    B. 8
    C. 9
    D. 10

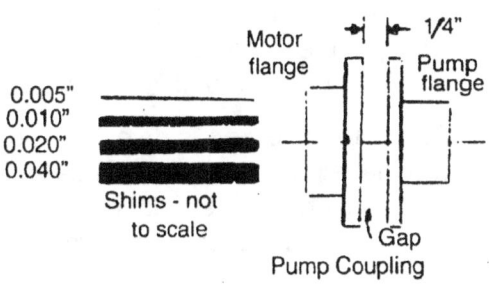

30.____

31. The dimension X on the keyway shown is
    A. 3 3/8"
    B. 3 9/16"
    C. 3 3/4"
    D. 4"

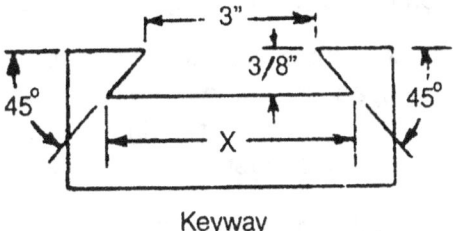

31.____

32. If the tank gage reads 120 psi, then the pipe gage should read _____ psi.
    A. 80
    B. 120
    C. 180
    D. 240

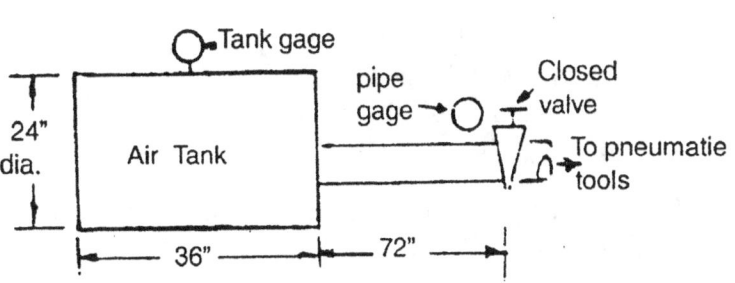

32.____

33. The MINIMUM number of feet of chainlink fence needed to completely enclose the storage yard shown is
    A. 278
    B. 286
    C. 295
    D. 304

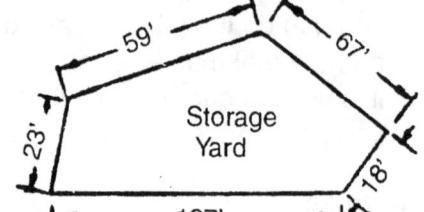

34. The distance X between the holes is
    A. 1 7/8"
    B. 2 1/16"
    C. 2 3/8"
    D. 2 9/16"

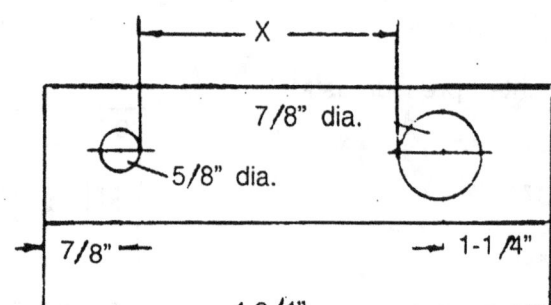

35. A rule of the Transit Authority is that all employees are required to report defective equipment to their superiors, even when the maintenance of the particular equipment is handled by someone else.
    The MAIN purpose of this rule is to
    A. determine who is doing his job improperly
    B. have repairs made before trouble occurs
    C. encourage all employees to be alert at all times
    D. reduce the cost of equipment

36. Some equipment is fitted with wing nuts.
    Such nuts are especially useful when
    A. the nut is to be wired closed
    B. space is limited
    C. the equipment is subject to vibration
    D. the nuts must be removed frequently

37. It is considered bad practice to use water to put out electrical fires MAINLY because the water may
    A. rust the equipment
    B. short circuit the lines
    C. cause a serious shock
    D. damage the electrical insulation

38. While you are being trained, you will be assigned to work with an experienced mechanic.
    It would be BEST for you to
    A. remind the mechanic that he is responsible for your training
    B. tell him frequently how much you know about the work
    C. let him do all the work while you observe closely
    D. be as cooperative and helpful as you can

39. The BEST instrument to use to make certain that two points, separated by a vertical distance of 9 feet, are in perfect vertical alignment is a   39.____

    A. square   B. level   C. plumb bob   D. protractor

40. If a measurement scaled from a drawing is one inch, and the scale of the drawing is 1/8-inch to the foot, then the one inch measurement would represent an actual length of   40.____

    A. 8 feet
    C. 1/8 of a foot
    B. 2 feet
    D. 8 inches

KEY (CORRECT ANSWERS)

1. B	11. B	21. C	31. C
2. B	12. B	22. D	32. B
3. A	13. B	23. D	33. D
4. B	14. C	24. D	34. A
5. B	15. D	25. A	35. B
6. C	16. A	26. D	36. D
7. D	17. D	27. A	37. C
8. D	18. D	28. D	38. D
9. B	19. C	29. B	39. C
10. C	20. D	30. A	40. A

TEST 2

DIRECTIONS: Each question or incomplete statement is followed by several suggested answers or completions. Select the one that BEST answers the question or completes the statement. *PRINT THE LETTER OF THE CORRECT ANSWER IN THE SPACE AT THE RIGHT.*

1. Cloth tapes should NOT be used when accurate measurements must be obtained because

    A. the numbers soon become worn and thus difficult to read
    B. there are not enough subdivisions of each inch on the tape
    C. the ink runs when wet, thus making the tape difficult to read
    D. small changes in the pull on the tape will make considerable differences in tape readings

2. It is considered good practice to release the pressure from an air hose before uncoupling the hose connection because this avoids

    A. wasting air
    B. possible personal injury
    C. damage to the air tool
    D. damage to the air compressor

3. In brick construction, a structural steel member is used to support the wall above door and window openings. This member is called a

    A. purlin   B. sill   C. truss   D. lintel

Questions 4-9.

DIRECTIONS: Questions 4 through 9 show the top view of an object in the first column, the front view of the same object in the second column and four drawings in the third column, one of which correctly represents the RIGHT side view of the object. Select the CORRECT right side view. As a guide, the first one is an illustrative example, the CORRECT answer of which is C.

Questions 10-14.

DIRECTIONS: Questions 10 through 14 are to be answered on the basis of the information contained in the safety regulations given below. In answering these questions, refer to these rules.

REGULATIONS FOR SMALL GROUPS WHO MOVE
FROM POINT TO POINT ON THE TRACKS

Employees who perform duties on the tracks in small groups and who move from point to point along the trainway must be on the alert at all times and prepared to clear the track when a train approaches without unnecessarily slowing it down. Underground at all times, and out-of-doors between sunset and sunrise, such employees must not enter upon the tracks unless each of them is equipped with an approved light. Flashlights must not be used for protection by such groups. Upon clearing the track to permit a train to pass, each member of the group must give a proceed signal, by hand or light, to the motorman of the train. Whenever such small groups are working in an area protected by caution lights or flags, but are not members of the gang for whom the flagging protection was established, they must not give proceed signals to motormen. The purpose of this rule is to avoid a motorman's confusing such signal with that of the flagman who is protecting a gang. Whenever a small group is engaged in work of an engrossing nature or at any time when the view of approaching trains is limited by reason of curves or otherwise, one man of the group, equipped with a whistle, must be assigned properly to warn and protect the man or men at work and must not perform any other duties while so assigned.

10. If a small group of men are traveling along the tracks toward their work location and a train approaches, they should

    A. stop the train
    B. signal the motorman to go slowly
    C. clear the track
    D. stop immediately

10.____

11. Small groups may enter upon the tracks

    A. only between sunset and sunrise
    B. provided each has an approved light
    C. provided their foreman has a good flashlight
    D. provided each man has an approved flashlight

11.____

12. After a small group has cleared the tracks in an area unprotected by caution lights or flags,

    A. each member must give the proceed signal to the motorman
    B. the foreman signals the motorman to proceed
    C. the motorman can proceed provided he goes slowly
    D. the last member off the tracks gives the signal to the motorman

12.____

13. If a small group is working in an area protected by the signals of a track gang, the members of the small group

    A. need not be concerned with train movement
    B. must give the proceed signal together with the track gang

13.____

C. can delegate one of their members to give the proceed signal
D. must not give the proceed signal

14. If the view of approaching trains is blocked, the small group should

    A. move to where they can see the trains
    B. delegate one of the group to warn and protect them
    C. keep their ears alert for approaching trains
    D. refuse to work at such locations

15. The information in an accident report which may be MOST useful in helping to prevent similar-type accidents from happening is the

    A. cause of the accident
    B. time of day it happened
    C. type of injuries suffered
    D. number of people injured

16. The MAIN reason why each coat of paint should be of a different color when two coats of paint are specified is that

    A. cheaper paint can be used as the undercoat
    B. less care need be taken in applying the coats
    C. any missed areas will be easier to spot
    D. the colors do not have to be exact

Questions 17-23.

DIRECTIONS: Questions 17 through 23 refer to the sketches shown to the right of each question.

17. The distance y is
    A. 5/8"
    B. 7/8"
    C. 1 1/8"
    D. 1 3/8"

18. The sketch shows the float-operated trippers for operating a sump pump. If you want the pump to start sooner, you should _____ tripper.
    A. *lower* the upper
    B. *lower* the lower
    C. *raise* the upper
    D. *raise* the lower

19. The width of the wood stud shown is
    A. 1 1/8"
    B. 1 5/16"
    C. 1 5/8"
    D. 3 5/8"

19.___

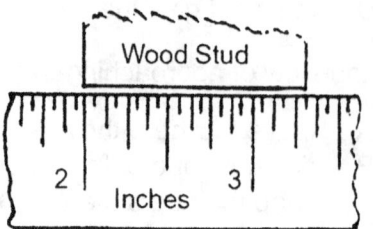

20. The right angle shown has been divided into four unequal parts.
    The number of degrees in angle X is
    A. 31°
    B. 33°
    C. 38°
    D. 45°

20.___

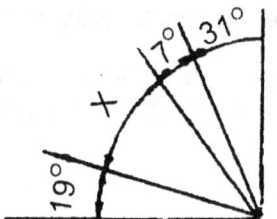

21. The reading on the meter shown is MOST NEARLY
    A. 0465
    B. 0475
    C. 0566
    D. 1566

21.___

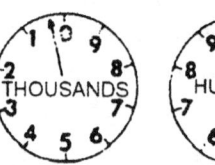

22. The length X of the slot shown is
    A. 2 3/8"
    B. 2 7/16"
    C. 2 1/2"
    D. 2 9/16"

22.___

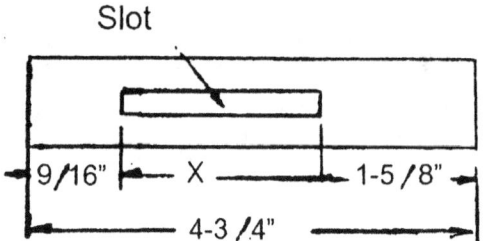

23. The volume of the bar shown is _____ cubic inches.
    A. 132
    B. 356
    C. 420
    D. 516

23.___

24. Gaskets should be used with

    A. flanged pipe fittings
    C. threaded reducing couplings
    B. bell and spigot pipe
    D. threaded bushings

24.___

25. The MAIN purpose for providing a plumbing fixture with a trap is to

   A. equalize the pressures in the drainage system
   B. catch any article that might plug the drain
   C. prevent passage of gases
   D. supply an easy means of cleaning if the fixture gets plugged

26. The *soil stack* of a drainage system is left open at its upper end in order to

   A. prevent the sewer from backing up into the traps
   B. prevent the siphoning of traps
   C. prevent ventilation of the drainage system
   D. hold a vacuum above the house drain line

27. Under the city color coding of pipes, drinking water pipes should be painted

   A. blue   B. yellow   C. green   D. red

28. When changing from a 2" pipe size to a 1" pipe in a horizontal steam line, the PROPER fitting to be used is a(n)

   A. concentric bushing
   B. face bushing
   C. concentric reducer
   D. eccentric reducer

29. An expansion slip joint

   A. permits longitudinal movement of a pipe
   B. is used when the pipe has been cut short
   C. compensates for differences in pipe pressure
   D. permits small movement for lining pipe hangers

30. The MAIN reason why brass is better than iron for water piping is that brass is

   A. cheaper
   B. lighter
   C. stronger
   D. more corrosion resistant

31. A bell and spigot cast iron pipe joint is made water-tight by

   A. rolling and beading the ends
   B. caulking with oakum and lead
   C. caulking with cotton wick and cement
   D. applying sealing compound to the threaded ends

32. The one of the following valves which is ALWAYS automatic in operation is the _____ valve.

   A. gate   B. angle   C. check   D. globe

33. Threaded joints may be made up tight by using pipe thread compound. The CORRECT procedure is to apply the compound

   A. only to the male threads
   B. only to the female threads
   C. to both male and female threads
   D. to either the male or female thread, depending on the pipe size

Questions 34-39.

DIRECTIONS: Questions 34 through 39 are to be answered on the basis of the riser diagram shown below.

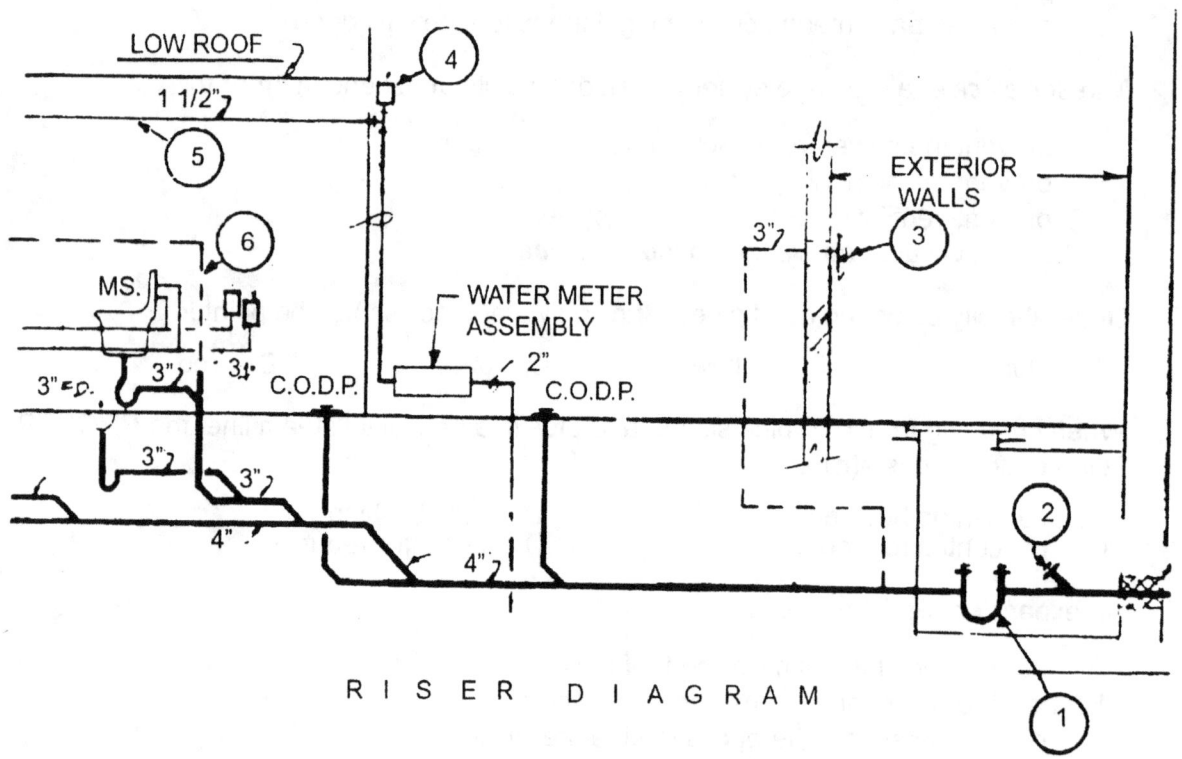

RISER DIAGRAM

34. Fitting 1 is a

   A. floor drain
   B. trap
   C. clean out
   D. check valve

35. Fitting 2 is a

   A. floor drain
   B. trap
   C. clean out
   D. check valve

36. Fitting 3 is a

   A. fire department connection
   B. sprinkler head
   C. valve
   D. fresh air inlet

37. Fitting 4 is a(n)

   A. gate valve
   B. air chamber
   C. running trap
   D. vent inlet

38. Line 5 is a

    A. hot water pipe
    B. vent line
    C. cold water line
    D. soil line

39. Line 6 is a _____ line.

    A. vent
    B. cold water
    C. hot water
    D. drain

40. A non-rising stem-type gate valve is especially useful when

    A. the stem must move downward only
    B. the pressure in the pipe must remain constant
    C. clearances around the valve are limited
    D. hand control of the valve is not required

KEY (CORRECT ANSWERS)

1.	D	11.	B	21.	A	31.	B
2.	B	12.	A	22.	D	32.	C
3.	D	13.	D	23.	C	33.	A
4.	C	14.	B	24.	A	34.	B
5.	A	15.	A	25.	C	35.	C
6.	C	16.	C	26.	B	36.	D
7.	B	17.	B	27.	C	37.	B
8.	B	18.	D	28.	D	38.	C
9.	C	19.	B	29.	A	39.	A
10.	C	20.	B	30.	D	40.	C

MECHANICAL APTITUDE
TOOL RECOGNITION AND USE
EXAMINATION SECTION
TEST 1

DIRECTIONS: Each question or incomplete statement is followed by several suggested answers or completions. Select the one that BEST answers the question or completes the statement. *PRINT THE LETTER OF THE CORRECT ANSWER IN THE SPACE AT THE RIGHT.*

Questions 1-16.

DIRECTIONS: Questions 1 through 16 refer to the tools shown below. The numbers in the answers refer to the numbers below the tools. NOTE: These tools are NOT shown to scale.

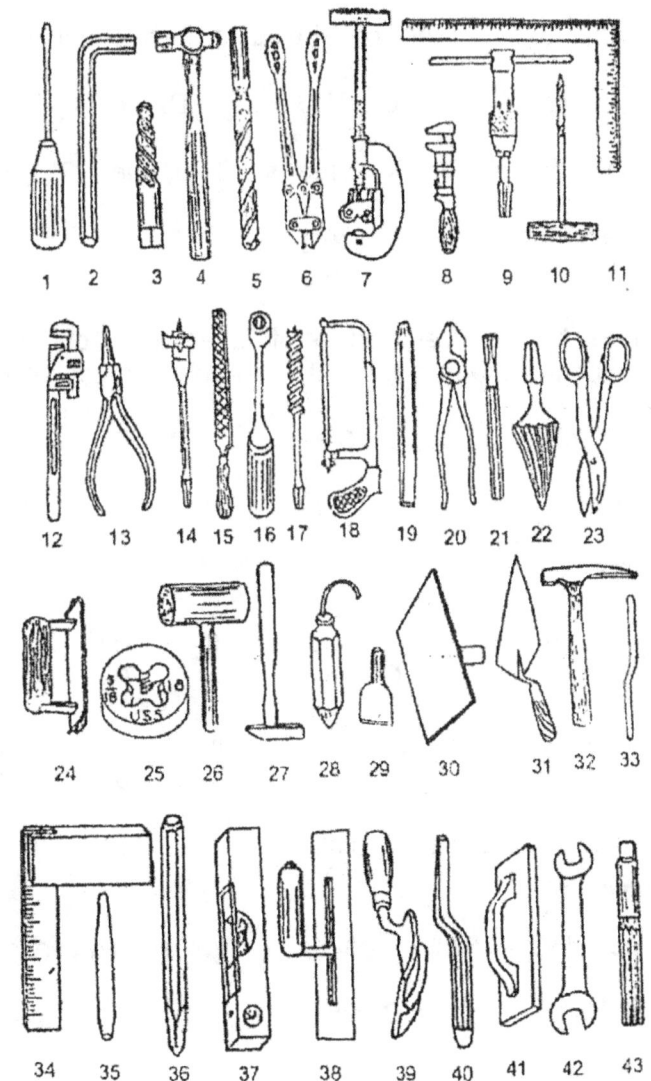

2 (#1)

1. In order to cut a piece of 5/16" diameter steel scaffold hoisting cable, you should use tool number
   A. 6   B. 7   C. 19   D. 23

   1._____

2. Scaffold planks are secured to joisting irons by means of lag screws.
   To properly tighten these lag screws, you should use tool number
   A. 12   B. 13   C. 20   D. 42

   2._____

3. While installing a steel angle iron lintel, you find that the threads on the embedded holding bolts are damaged.
   You should repair the threads by using tool number
   A. 7   B. 9   C. 25   D. 43

   3._____

4. It is necessary to cut a hole in a concrete foundation wall in order to place a small bolt.
   To cut this small hole, you should use tool number
   A. 14   B. 19   C. 21   D. 40

   4._____

5. If tool number 17 bears the mark "7," this tool should be used to drill holes having a diameter of
   A. 7/64"   B. 7/32"   C. 7/16"   D. 7/8"

   5._____

6. If the marking on the blade of tool number 18 reads "10-18," the "18" refers to the
   A. number of teeth per inch   B. weight
   C. thickness   D. length

   6._____

7. If two points are separated by a vertical distance of 12 feet, the tool that should be used to make certain that the points are in perfect vertical alignment is number
   A. 11   B. 28   C. 34   D. 37

   7._____

8. A 3/4" diameter hole must be made in a steel floor beam.
   The tool you should use is number
   A. 3   B. 5   C. 9   D. 22

   8._____

9. To cut the corner off a building brick, you should use tool number
   A. 4   B. 27   C. 29   D. 36

   9._____

10. A 2" x 2" x 3/16" steel angle should be cut using tool number
    A. 6   B. 7   C. 18   D. 19

    10._____

11. The term "snips" should be applied to tool number
    A. 6   B. 13   C. 20   D. 23

    11._____

12. To line-up the bolt holes in two structural steel beams, you should use tool number
    A. 1   B. 33   C. 35   D. 36

    12._____

13. A "hawk" is tool number   13.____
    A. 29   B. 30   C. 38   D. 41

14. After an 8" thick brick wall has been erected, it is discovered that a hole   14.____
    should have been left for a 4" sewer pipe.
    To cut that hole, you should use tool number
    A. 5   B. 19   C. 32   D. 36

15. A "float" is tool number   15.____
    A. 30   B. 31   C. 33   D. 41

16. A "Stillson" is tool number   16.____
    A. 2   B. 8   C. 12   D. 22

KEY (CORRECT ANSWERS)

1.	A	11.	D
2.	D	12.	C
3.	C	13.	B
4.	C	14.	D
5.	C	15.	D
6.	A	16.	C
7.	B		
8.	B		
9.	C		
10.	C		

TEST 2

DIRECTIONS: Each question or incomplete statement is followed by several suggested answers or completions. Select the one that BEST answers the question or completes the statement. *PRINT THE LETTER OF THE CORRECT ANSWER IN THE SPACE AT THE RIGHT.*

1. The stake shown in the sketch at the right is a _____ stake.
   A. hatchet
   B. conductor
   C. solid mandrel
   D. beak horn

   1._____

2. When a circle is too large to be drawn with a pair of dividers, the PROPER tool to use is a
   A. trammel
   B. protractor
   C. combination set
   D. flexible curve

   2._____

3. A rivet set is a tool used to
   A. shape the head of a rivet
   B. mark off the spacing of rivets
   C. remove a loose rivet
   D. check the shank length of a rivet

   3._____

4. The hammer shown in the sketch at the right is a _____ hammer.
   A. raising
   B. ball peen
   C. setting
   D. cross-over

   4._____

5. Of the following, the BEST tool to use to scribe a line parallel to the straight edge of a piece of sheet metal is a(n)
   A. outside caliper
   B. pair of dividers
   C. template
   D. scratch gage

   5._____

6. Of the following, the BEST device to use to check the condition of the insulation of a cable is the
   A. ohmmeter
   B. wheatstone bridge
   C. voltmeter
   D. megger

   6._____

7. Of the following fittings, the one used to connect two lengths of conduit in a straight line is a(n)
   A. elbow   B. nipple   C. tee   D. coupling

   7._____

8. If a nut is to be tightened to an exact specified value, the wrench that should be used is a(n) _____ wrench.
   A. torque   B. lock-jaw   C. alligator   D. spaner

   8._____

9. A stillson wrench is also called a _____ wrench.
   A. strap B. pipe C. monkey D. crescent

10. A machine screw is indicated on a drawing as . The head is the American Standard type called
    A. flat
    B. oval
    C. fillister
    D. round

11. The tool that is shown at the right is properly referred to as a(n) _____ tap.
    A. bottoming
    B. acme
    C. taper
    D. plug

12. The tool indicated at the right is referred to as an Arc Punch. This tool should be used to
    A. cut holes in 1/16" steel
    B. cut large diameter holes in masonry
    C. run through a conduit prior to pulling a cable or wires
    D. make holes in rubber or leather gasket material

13. The plumbing fitting shown at the right is called a
    A. street elbow
    B. return bend
    C. running trap
    D. reversing "el"

14. For which one of the following uses would it be unsafe to use a carpenter's hammer?
    A. casing mail   B. hand punch
    C. hardened steel surface D. plastic surface

15. Of the following, the MAIN advantage in using a Phillips head screw is that
    A. the threads of the Phillips head screw have a deeper bite than standard screw threads
    B. the screwdriver used on this type of screw is more likely to keep its edge than a standard screwdriver
    C. a single screwdriver fits all size screws of this type
    D. the screwdriver used on this type of screw is less likely to slip than a standard screwdriver

16. One of the reasons why a polyester rope is considered to be the BEST general purpose rope is that it
    A. does not stretch as much as ropes made of other materials
    B. is available in longer lengths than ropes made of other materials
    C. does not fray as much as ropes made of other materials
    D. contains more strands than ropes made of other materials

16._____

17. The PROPER saw to use to cut wood with the grain is a _____ saw.
    A. hack   B. crosscut   C. back   D. rip

17._____

18. Assume that the instruction manual for a machine indicates that a certain bolt must be tightened with a specified amount of force.
    Of the following tools, the one which should be used to tighten the bolt with the specified amount of force is a(n) _____ wrench.
    A. torque   B. adjustable   C. stillson   D combination

18._____

19. The power source of a pneumatic tool is
    A. manual
    B. water pressure
    C. compressed air
    D. electricity

19._____

20. The tool used to cut internal pipe threads is a
    A. broach   B. tap   C. die   D. rod

20._____

KEY (CORRECT ANSWERS)

1.	A	11.	A
2.	A	12.	D
3.	A	13.	B
4.	C	14.	C
5.	D	15.	D
6.	D	16.	A
7.	D	17.	D
8.	A	18.	A
9.	B	19.	C
10.	B	20.	B

READING COMPREHENSION
UNDERSTANDING AND INTERPRETING WRITTEN MATERIAL
EXAMINATION SECTION
TEST 1

DIRECTIONS: Each question or incomplete statement is followed by several suggested answers or completions. Select the one that BEST answers the question or completes the statement. *PRINT THE LETTER OF THE CORRECT ANSWER IN THE SPACE AT THE RIGHT.*

Questions 1-8.

DIRECTIONS: Questions 1 through 8, inclusive, are to be answered in accordance with the following information.

In his 2017 annual report to the Mayor, the Public Works Commissioner stated that the city's basic water pollution control program begun in 1981 and costing $425 million so far would be completed in five or six years at a cost of $275 million more. However, he said, the city must spend an additional $175 million more on its marginal pollution control program to protect present and proposed beaches. Under the basic program, the city will have eliminated the last major discharges of raw sewage into the harbor. Over 800 million gallons, two-thirds of the city's spent water each day, is now treated at 12 plants, to which six new plants will be added, enabling the city to treat the estimated 1.8 billion gallons that will be discharged daily in 2050. The department had about $200 million worth of municipal construction under way in 2017, and completed $85.5 millions' worth.

1. According to the above, the city will add _____ new plants.
    A. 18   B. 12   C. 6   D. 4

2. The amount of municipal construction under way in 2017 was _____ million.
    A. $85.5   B. $175   C. $200   D. $425

3. It is estimated that in 2050 the city will treat daily _____ gallons.
    A. 700 million B. 800 million C. 900 million D. 1.8 billion

4. According to the above article, the total cost of the water pollution program begun in 1981 will be _____ million.
    A. $275   B. $425   C. $700   D. $815

5. According to the above article, to protect present and proposed beaches, the city must spend an additional _____ million.
    A. $175   B. $275   C. $425   D. $450

6. The above article concerns the statements of the Commissioner of Public Works in his _____ annual report to the Mayor.
    A. 1981   B. 2050   C. 2017   D. 2018

7. The word *discharged* as used in the above article means MOST NEARLY 7.____

   A. emitted B. erased C. refuted D. repelled

8. The word *pollution* as used in the above article means MOST NEARLY 8.____

   A. condensation B. purification
   C. contamination D. distillation

Questions 9-15.

DIRECTIONS: Questions 9 through 15, inclusive, are to be answered in accordance with the following information.

At sea level the atmosphere can exert a pressure of 14.7 pounds per square inch. This pressure is capable of sustaining a column of water having a height equal to 14.7 pounds multiplied by 2.304 (the height of water in feet which will exert one pound per square inch pressure). No pump built can produce a perfect vacuum. The atmospheric pressure exerting its force on the surface of the water from which suction is being taken forces the water up through the suction to the pump. From this, it is evident that the maximum height which a water pump of this type can lift water is determined ultimately by the atmospheric pressure. The tightness of the pump and its ability to create a vacuum also have a bearing.

9. The meaning of the word *vacuum* as used in the above article is a 9.____

   A. space entirely devoid of matter
   B. sealed tube filled with gas
   C. bottle-shaped vessel with a double wall
   D. cleaning device

10. With reference to the above article, if a pump could produce a perfect vacuum, the MAXIMUM height, in feet, that it could lift water at sea level is MOST NEARLY 10.____

    A. 33.9 B. 29.4 C. 23.3 D. 14.7

11. With reference to the above article, a column of water having a height of 4.6 feet at sea level will exert a pressure of MOST NEARLY _____ pounds per square inch. 11.____

    A. 3 B. 2 C. 1 D. $\frac{1}{2}$

12. The word *atmosphere* as used in the above article means 12.____

    A. the pull of gravity
    B. perfect vacuum
    C. the whole mass of air surrounding the earth
    D. the weight of water at sea level

13. The word *bearing* as used in the above article means MOST NEARLY 13.____

    A. direction B. connection
    C. divergence D. convergence

14. The word *evident* as used in the above article means MOST NEARLY   14.____

    A. disconcerting   B. obscure
    C. equivocal   D. manifest

15. The word *maximum* as used in the above article means MOST NEARLY   15.____

    A. best   B. median   C. adjacent   D. greatest

Questions 16-19.

DIRECTIONS: Questions 16 through 19, inclusive, are to be answered in accordance with the following paragraph.

One of the categories of nuisance is a chemical one and relates to the dissolved oxygen of the watercourse. The presence in sewage and industrial wastes of materials capable of undergoing biochemical oxidation and resulting in reduction of oxygen in the watercourse leads to a partial or complete depletion of this oxygen. This, in turn, leads to the subsequent production of malodorous products of decomposition, to the destruction of aquatic plant life and major fish life, and to conditions offensive to sight and smell.

16. The word *malodorous* as used in the above paragraph means MOST NEARLY   16.____

    A. fragrant   B. fetid   C. wholesome   D. redolent

17. From the above paragraph, because of pollution the amount of dissolved oxygen in the waterways is   17.____

    A. released   B. multiplied
    C. lessened   D. saturated

18. The word *categories* as used in the above paragraph means MOST NEARLY   18.____

    A. divisions   B. clubs   C. symbols   D. products

19. The word *offensive* as used in the above paragraph means MOST NEARLY   19.____

    A. pliable   B. complaint
    C. deferential   D. disagreeable

Questions 20-22.

DIRECTIONS: Questions 20 through 22, inclusive, are to be answered in accordance with the following paragraph.

Thermostats should be tested in hot water for proper opening. A bucket should be filled with sufficient water to cover the thermostat and fitted with a thermometer suspended in the water so that the sensitive bulb portion does not rest directly on the bucket. The water is then heated on a stove. As the temperature of the water passes the 160-165° range, the thermostat should start to open and should be completely opened when the temperature has risen to 185-190°. Lifting the thermostat into the air should cause a pronounced closing action, and the unit should be closed entirely within a short time.

20. The thermostat described above is a device which opens and closes with changes in the

    A. position
    B. pressure
    C. temperature
    D. surroundings

21. According to the above paragraph, the closing action of the thermostat should be tested by

    A. working the thermostat back and forth
    B. permitting the water to cool gradually
    C. adding cold water to the bucket
    D. removing the thermostat from the bucket

22. The bulb of the thermometer should NOT rest directly on the bucket because

    A. the bucket gets hotter than the water
    B. the thermometer might be damaged in that position
    C. it is difficult to read the thermometer in that position
    D. the thermometer might interfere with operation of the thermostat

Questions 23-25.

DIRECTIONS: Questions 23 through 25, inclusive, are to be answered in accordance with information given in the paragraph below.

All idle pumps should be turned daily by hand and should be run under power at least once a week. Whenever repairs are made on a pump, a record should be kept so that it will be possible to judge the success with which the pump is performing its functions. If a pump fails to deliver liquid, there may be an obstruction in the suction line, the pump's parts may be badly worn, or the packing defective.

23. According to the above paragraph, pumps

    A. in use should be turned by hand every day
    B. which are not in use should be run under power every day
    C. which are in daily use should be run under power several times a week
    D. which are not in use should be turned by hand every day

24. According to the above paragraph, the reason for keeping records of repairs made on pumps is to

    A. make certain that proper maintenance is being performed
    B. discover who is responsible for improper repairs
    C. rate the performance of the pumps
    D. know when to replace worn parts

25. The one of the following causes of pump failure which is NOT mentioned in the above paragraph is

    A. excessive suction lift
    B. clogged lines
    C. bad packing
    D. worn parts

KEY (CORRECT ANSWERS)

1.	C	11.	B
2.	C	12.	C
3.	D	13.	B
4.	C	14.	D
5.	A	15.	D
6.	C	16.	B
7.	A	17.	C
8.	C	18.	A
9.	A	19.	D
10.	A	20.	C

21. D
22. A
23. D
24. C
25. A

TEST 2

DIRECTIONS: Each question or incomplete statement is followed by several suggested answers or completions. Select the one that BEST answers the question or completes the statement. *PRINT THE LETTER OF THE CORRECT ANSWER IN THE SPACE AT THE RIGHT.*

Questions 1-2.

DIRECTIONS: Questions 1 and 2 are to be answered in accordance with the information given in the following paragraph.

A sludge lagoon is an excavated area in which digested sludge is desired. Lagoon depths vary from six to eight feet. There are no established criteria for the required capacity of a lagoon. The sludge moisture content is reduced by evaporation and drainage. Volume reduction is slow, especially in cold and rainy weather. Weather and soil conditions affect concentration. The drying period ranges from a period of several months to several years. After the sludge drying period has ended, a bulldozer or tractor can be used to remove the sludge. The dried sludge can be used for fill of low ground. A filled dried lagoon can be developed into a lawn. Lagoons can be used for emergency storage when the sludge beds are full. Lagoons are popular because they are inexpensive to build and operate. They have a disadvantage of being unsightly. A hazard to lagoon operation is the possibility of draining partly digested sludge to the lagoon that creates a fly and odor nuisance.

1. In accordance with the given paragraph, sludge lagoons have the disadvantage of being   1.___

    A. unsightly   B. too deep
    C. concentrated   D. wet

2. In accordance with the given paragraph, moisture content is reduced by   2.___

    A. digestion   B. evaporation
    C. oxidation   D. removal

Questions 3-5.

DIRECTIONS: Questions 3 through 5, inclusive, should be answered in accordance with the following paragraph.

Sharpening a twist drill by hand is a skill that is mastered only after much practice and careful attention to the details. Therefore, whenever possible, use a tool grinder in which the drills can be properly positioned, clamped in place, and set with precision for the various angles. This machine grinding will enable you to sharpen the drills accurately. As a result, they will last longer and will produce more accurate holes.

3. According to the above paragraph, one reason for sharpening drills accurately is that the drills   3.___

    A. can then be used in a hand drill as well as a drill press
    B. will last longer
    C. can then be used by unskilled persons
    D. cost less

4. According to the above paragraph,

   A. it is easier to sharpen a drill by machine than by hand
   B. drills cannot be sharpened by hand
   C. only a skilled mechanic can learn to sharpen a drill by hand
   D. a good mechanic will learn to sharpen drills by hand

5. As used in the above paragraph, the word *precision* means MOST NEARLY

   A. accuracy   B. ease   C. rigidity   D. speed

Questions 6-9.

DIRECTIONS: Questions 6 through 9, inclusive, should be answered in accordance with the following paragraph.

    Centrifugal pumps have relatively fewer moving parts than reciprocating pumps, and no valves. While reciprocating pumps when new are usually more efficient than centrifugal pumps, the latter retain their efficiency longer. Most rotary pumps are also without valves, but they have closely meshing parts between which high pressures may be set up after they begin to wear. In general, centrifugal pumps can be made much smaller than reciprocating pumps giving the same result. There is an exception in that positive displacement pumps delivering small volumes at high heads are smaller than equivalent centrifugal pumps. Centrifugal pumps cost less when first purchased than other comparable pumps. The original outlay may be as little as one-third or one-half that of a reciprocating pump suitable for the same purpose.

6. The type of pump NOT mentioned in the above paragraph is the _____ type.

   A. rotary   B. propeller
   C. reciprocating   D. centrifugal

7. According to the above paragraph, the type of pump that sometimes has valves and sometimes does NOT is the

   A. rotary   B. propeller
   C. reciprocating   D. centrifugal

8. According to the above paragraph, centrifugal pumps are

   A. *always* smaller than reciprocating pumps
   B. *smaller* than reciprocating pumps only when designed to deliver small quantities at low pressures
   C. *larger* than reciprocating pumps only when designed to deliver small quantities at high pressures
   D. *larger* than reciprocating pumps only when designed to deliver large quantities at low pressures

9. The advantage of centrifugal pumps that is NOT mentioned in the above paragraph is that

   A. the centrifugal pump retains its efficiency longer
   B. it is impossible to create an excessive pressure when using a centrifugal pump

C. there are fewer parts to wear out in a centrifugal pump
D. the centrifugal pump is cheaper

Questions 10-12.

DIRECTIONS: Questions 10 through 12, inclusive, should be answered in accordance with the following paragraph.

Gaskets made of relatively soft materials are placed between the meeting surfaces of hydraulic fittings in order to increase the tightness of the seal. They should be composed of materials that will not be affected by the liquid to be enclosed, nor by the conditions under which the system operates, including maximum pressure and temperature. They should be able to maintain the amount of clearance required between meeting surfaces. One of the materials most widely used in making gaskets is neoprene. Since neoprene is flexible, it is often used in sheet form at points where a gasket must expand enough to allow air to accumulate, as with cover plates on supply tanks. Over a period of time, oil tends to deteriorate the material used in making neoprene gaskets. The condition of the gasket must, therefore, be checked whenever the unit is disassembled. Since neoprene gasket material is soft and flexible, it easily becomes misshapen, scratched or torn. Great care is therefore necessary in handling neoprene. Shellac, gasket sealing compounds or *pipe dope* should never be used with sheet neoprene, unless absolutely necessary for satisfactory installation.

10. Of the following, the one that is NOT mentioned in the above paragraph as a requirement for a good gasket material is that the material must be

    A. cheap
    B. unaffected by heat developed in a system
    C. relatively soft
    D. capable of maintaining required clearances

10.___

11. According to the above paragraph, neoprene will be affected by

    A. air B. temperature C. pressure D. oil

11.___

12. According to the above paragraph, care is necessary in handling neoprene because

    A. its condition must be checked frequently
    B. it tears easily
    C. pipe dope should not be used
    D. it is difficult to use

12.___

Questions 13-15.

DIRECTIONS: Questions 13 through 15, inclusive, are to be answered in accordance with the information given in the paragraph below.

Some gases which may be inhaled have an irritant effect on the respiratory tract. Among them are ammonia fumes, hydrogen sulfide, nitrous fumes, and phosgene. Persons who have been exposed to irritant gases must lie down at once and keep absolutely quiet until the dotor arrives. The action of some of these gases may be delayed, and at first the victim may show few or no symptoms.

13. According to the above paragraph, the part of the body that is MOST affected by irritant gases is the

    A. heart B. lungs C. skin D. nerves

14. According to the above paragraph, a person who has inhaled an irritant gas should be

    A. given artificial respiration
    B. made to rest
    C. wrapped in blankets
    D. made to breathe smelling salts

15. A person is believed to have come in contact with an irritant gas but he does not become sick immediately.
    According to the above paragraph, we may conclude that the person

    A. did not really come in contact with the gas
    B. will become sick later
    C. came in contact with a small amount of gas
    D. may possibly become sick later

Questions 16-22.

DIRECTIONS: Questions 16 through 22, inclusive, are to be answered in accordance with the following paragraph.

At 2:30 P.M. on Monday, October 25, Mr. Paul Jones, a newly appointed sewage treatment worker, started on a routine inspectional tour of the settling tanks and other sewage treatment works installations of the plant to which he was assigned. At 2:33 P.M., Mr. Jones discovered a co-worker, Mr. James P. Brown, lying unconscious on the ground. Mr. Jones quickly reported the facts to his immediate superior, Mr. Jack Rota, who immediately telephoned for an ambulance. Mr. Rota then rushed to the site and placed a heavy woolen blanket over the victim. Mr. Brown was taken to the Ave. H hospital by an ambulance driven by Mr. Dave Smith, which arrived at the sewage disposal plant at 3:02 P.M. Patrolman Robert Daly, badge number 12520, had arrived before the ambulance and recorded all the details of the incident, including the statements of Mr. Jones, Mr. Rota, and Mr. Nick Nespola, a Stationary Engineer (Electric), who stated that he saw the victim when he fell to the ground.

16. The time which elapsed between the start of the sewage treatment worker's routine inspection and the arrival of the ambulance was MOST NEARLY _____ minutes.

    A. 3 B. 28 C. 29 D. 32

17. The name of the sewage treatment worker's immediate superior was

    A. James P. Brown   B. Jack Rota
    C. Paul Jones   D. Robert Daly

18. The name of the patrolman was

    A. James P. Brown   B. Jack Rota
    C. Paul Jones   D. Robert Daly

19. Referring to the above, the incident occurred on

    A. Monday, Oct. 25
    B. Monday, Oct. 26
    C. Tuesday, Oct. 25
    D. Tuesday, Oct. 26

20. The victim was found at exactly

    A. 2:30 A.M.   B. 2:33 P.M.   C. 2:33 A.M.   D. 2:30 P.M.

21. The sewage treatment worker's name was

    A. James P. Brown
    B. Jack Rota
    C. Paul Jones
    D. Dave Smith

22. The man named Nick Nespola was the

    A. Stationary Engineer (Electric)
    B. patrolman
    C. victim
    D. ambulance driver

Questions 23-25.

DIRECTIONS: Questions 23 through 25, inclusive, are to be answered in accordance with the information given in the paragraph below.

The bearings of all electrical equipment should be subjected to careful inspection at scheduled periodic intervals in order to secure maximum life. The newer type of sleeve bearings requires very little attention since the oil does not become contaminated and oil leakage is negligible. Maintenance of the correct oil level is frequently the only upkeep required for years of service with this type of bearing.

23. According to the above paragraph, the MAIN reason for making periodic inspections of electrical equipment is to

    A. reduce waste of lubricants
    B. prevent injury to operators
    C. make equipment last longer
    D. keep operators *on their toes*

24. According to the above paragraph, the bearings of electrical equipment should be inspected

    A. whenever the equipment isn't working properly
    B. whenever there is time for inspections
    C. at least once a year
    D. at regular times

25. According to the above paragraph, when using newer type of sleeve bearings,

    A. oil leakage is slight
    B. the oil level should be checked every few years
    C. oil leakage is due to carelessness
    D. oil soon becomes dirty

KEY (CORRECT ANSWERS)

1.	A	11.	D
2.	B	12.	B
3.	B	13.	B
4.	A	14.	B
5.	A	15.	D
6.	B	16.	D
7.	A	17.	B
8.	C	18.	D
9.	B	19.	A
10.	A	20.	B

21. C
22. A
23. C
24. D
25. A

TEST 3

DIRECTIONS: Each question or incomplete statement is followed by several suggested answers or completions. Select the one that BEST answers the question or completes the statement. *PRINT THE LETTER OF THE CORRECT ANSWER IN THE SPACE AT THE RIGHT.*

Questions 1-2.

DIRECTIONS: Questions 1 and 2 are to be answered on the basis of the paragraph below.

When summers are hot and dry, much water will be used for watering lawns. Domestic use will be further increased by more bathing, while public use will be affected by much street sprinkling and use in parks and recreation fields for watering grass and for ornamental fountains. Variations in the weather may cause variations in water consumption. A succession of showers in the summer could significantly reduce water consumption. High temperatures may also lead to high water use for air conditioning purposes. On the other hand, in cold weather water may be wasted at the faucets to prevent freezing of pipes, thereby greatly increasing consumption.

1. According to the above passage, water consumption

   A. will not be affected by the weather to any appreciable extent
   B. will always increase in the warm weather and decrease in cold weather
   C. will increase in cold weather and decrease in warm weather
   D. may increase because of high or low temperatures

2. The MAIN subject of the above passage is

   A. climatic conditions affecting water consumption
   B. water consumption in arid regions
   C. conservation of water
   D. weather variations

Questions 3-4.

DIRECTIONS: Questions 3 and 4 are to be answered on the basis of the paragraph below.

The efficiency of the water works management will affect con-sumption by decreasing loss and waste. Leaks in the water mains and services and unauthorized use of water can be kept to a minimum by surveys. A water supply that is both safe and attractive in quality will be used to a greater extent than one of poor quality. In this connection, it should be recognized that improvement of the quality of water supply will probably be followed by an increase in consumption. Increasing the pressure will have a similar effect. Changing the rates charged for water will also affect consumption. A study found that consumption decreases about five percent for each ten percent increase in water rates. Similarly, water consumption increases when the water rates are decreasing.

3. According to the above passage, an increase in the quality of water would MOST LIKELY

   A. cause an increase in water consumption
   B. decrease water consumption by about 10%

C. cause a decrease in water consumption
D. have no effect on water consumption

4. According to the above passage, a ten percent decrease in water rates would MOST LIKELY result in a _____ in the water consumption.

   A. five percent decrease
   B. five percent increase
   C. ten percent decrease
   D. ten percent increase

Questions 5-6.

DIRECTIONS: Questions 5 and 6 are to be answered on the basis of the paragraph below.

While the average domestic use of water may be expected to be about 35 gallons per person daily, wide variations are found. These are largely dependent upon the economic status of the consumers and will differ greatly in various sections of the city. In the high value residential districts of a city or in a suburban community of similar type population, the water consumption per person will be high. In apartment houses, which may be considered as representing the maximum domestic demand to be expected, the average consumption should be about 60 gallons per person. In an area of high value single residences, even higher consumption may be expected since to the ordinary domestic demand there will be added amount for watering lawns. The slum districts of large cities will show a consumption per person of about 20 gallons daily. The lowest figures of all will be found in low value districts where sewerage is not available and where perhaps a single faucet serves one or several households.

5. According to the above passage, domestic water consumption per person

   A. would probably be lowest for persons in an area of high value single residences
   B. would probably be lowest for persons in an apartment house
   C. would probably be lowest for persons in a slum area
   D. does not depend at all upon area or income

6. According to the above passage, the water consumption in apartment houses as compared to slum houses is about _____ times as much.

   A. $1\frac{1}{2}$
   B. 2
   C. $2\frac{1}{2}$
   D. 3

Questions 7-9.

DIRECTIONS: Questions 7 through 9 are to be answered in accordance with the paragraph below.

A connection for commercial purposes may be made from a metered fire or sprinkler line of 4 inches or larger in diameter, provided a meter is installed on the commercial branch line. Such connection shall be taken from the inlet side of the fire meter control valve, and the method of connection shall be subject to the approval of the department. On a 4-inch fire line, the connection shall not exceed inches in diameter. On a fire line 6 inches or larger in diameter, the size of the connection shall not exceed 2 inches. Fire lines shall not be cross-connected with any system of piping within the building.

7. According to the above paragraph, a connection for commercial purposes may be made to a metered sprinkler line provided that the diameter of the sprinkler line is AT LEAST

   A. $1\frac{1}{2}"$ B. 2"   C. 4"   D. 6"

8. According to the above paragraph, the connection for commercial purposes is taken from the

   A. inlet side of the main control valve
   B. outlet side of the wet connection
   C. inlet side of the fire meter control valve
   D. outlet side of the Siamese

9. According to the above paragraph, the MAXIMUM size permitted for the connection for commercial purposes depends on the

   A. location of the fire meter valve
   B. use to which the commercial line is to be put
   C. method of connection to the sprinkler line
   D. size of the sprinkler line

Questions 10-11.

DIRECTIONS: Questions 10 and 11 are to be answered in accordance with the paragraph below.

Meters shall be set or reset so that they may be easily examined and read. In all premises where the supply of water is to be fully metered, the meter shall be set within three feet of the building or vault wall at. point of entry of service pipe. The service pipe between meter control valve and meter shall be kept exposed. When a building is situated back of the building line or conditions exist in a building that prevent the setting of the meter at a point of entry, meter may be set outside of the building in a proper watertight and frost-proof pit or meter box, or at another location approved by the Deputy Commissioner, Assistant to Commissioner, or the Chief Inspector.

10. According to the above paragraph, a meter should be set

    A. at a point in the building convenient to the owner
    B. within 3 feet of the building wall
    C. in back of the building
    D. where the district inspector thinks is best

11. According to the above paragraph, one of the conditions imposed when a meter is permitted to be installed outside of a building is that the meter must be installed

    A. between the service pipe and the meter control valve
    B. within 3 feet of the point of entry of the service pipe
    C. in a watertight enclosure
    D. above ground in a frost-proof box

Questions 12-15.

DIRECTIONS: Questions 12 through 15 are to be answered in accordance with the paragraphs below.

No individual or collective air conditioning system installed on any premises for a single consumer shall be permitted to waste annually more than the equivalent of a continuous flow of five gallons of city water per minute.

All individual or collective air conditioning systems installed on any premises for a single consumer using city water annually in excess of the equivalent of five gallons per minute shall be equipped with a water conserving device such as economizer, evaporative condenser, water cooling tower, or other similar apparatus, which device shall not consume for makeup purposes in excess of 15% of the consumption that would normally be used without such device.

Any individual or collective group of such units installed on any premises for a single consumer with a rated capacity of 25 tons or more, or water consumption of 50 gallons or more per minute, shall be equipped, where required by the department, with a water meter to separately register the consumption of such unit or groups of units.

This rule shall also apply to all air conditioning equipment now in service.

12. The rules described in the above paragraphs apply

    A. *only* to new installations of air conditioning equipment
    B. *only* to air conditioning systems which waste more than 5 gallons of city water per minute
    C. *only* to new installations of air conditioning equipment which waste more than 5 gallons of city water per minute
    D. to all air conditioning systems, whether existing ones or new installations

13. According to the above paragraphs, one of the acceptable methods of reducing wasting of water in an air conditioning system is by means of a

    A. cooling tower   B. water meter
    C. check valve   D. collective system

14. According to the above paragraphs, the department may require that an air conditioning system have a separate water meter when the system

    A. wastes more than 5 gallons of city water per minute
    B. uses more than 15% make-up water
    C. is equipped with an economizer
    D. has a rated capacity of 25 tons or more

15. According to the above paragraphs, the MAXIMUM quantity of make-up water permitted where an air conditioning system uses 50 gallons of water per minute is _____ gallons/minute.

    A. 7   B. $7\frac{1}{2}$ C. 8   D. $8\frac{1}{2}$

Questions 16-17.

DIRECTIONS: Questions 16 and 17 are to be answered in accordance with the paragraph below.

Where flushometers, suction tanks, other fixtures or piping are equipped with quick closing valves and are supplied by direct street pressure in excess of 70 pounds, an air chamber of an approved type shall be installed within two feet of the house control valve or meter in the service near the point of entry. Where water hammer conditions exist in any installation, regardless of the pressure obtaining, an air chamber of an approved type shall be installed where and as directed by the Chief Inspector or Engineer.

16. According to the above paragraph, air chambers are required when or wherever

    A. there are flushometers
    B. piping is supplied at a direct street pressure in excess of 70 lbs. per sq. in.
    C. a quick closing valve is used
    D. water hammer can occur in any piping

17. According to the above paragraph, air chambers should be installed

    A. within two feet of the house control valve or meter
    B. in a water system regardless of operating pressure
    C. on the fixture side of the quick closing valve
    D. on the suction side of the service meter

Questions 18-23.

DIRECTIONS: Questions 18 through 23 are to be answered in accordance with the paragraph below.

The acceptor's responsibility—The purpose of commercial standards is to establish for specific commodities, nationally *recognized* grades or consumer *criteria* and the benefits therefrom will be measurable in direct proportion to their general recognition and actual use. Instances will occur when it may be necessary to deviate from the standard, and the signing of an acceptance does not *preclude* such departures; however, such signature indicates an *intention* to follow the commercial standard where practicable, in the production, distribution, or consumption of the article in question.

18. The advantage which may be gained from the establishment of commercial standards is dependent upon the

    A. degree of consumer and manufacturer acceptance
    B. improvement of product quality
    C. degree of change required in the manufacturing process
    D. establishment and use of the highest standards

19. Nationally respected and adopted commercial standards are

    A. *undesirable;* as they are a direct benefit to unscrupulous manufacturers
    B. *desirable;* as they serve as a yardstick for consumers
    C. *undesirable;* as they tend to lower quality
    D. *desirable;* as they tend to reduce manufacturing costs

20. The word *preclude,* as used in this paragraph, means MOST NEARLY

    A. permit   B. allow   C. include   D. prevent

21. The word *intention,* as used in this paragraph, means MOST NEARLY

    A. agreement   B. impulse   C. objection   D. obstinance

22. The word *recognized,* as used in this paragraph, means MOST NEARLY

    A. desirable   B. stable   C. branded   D. accepted

23. The word *criteria,* as used in this paragraph, means MOST NEARLY

    A. efforts   B. standards   C. usage   D. costs

Questions 24-25.

DIRECTIONS: Questions 24 and 25 are to be answered in accordance with the paragraph below.

Sewage treatment plants are designed so that the sewage flow reaches the plant by gravity. In some instances, a small percentage of the sewerage system may be below the planned level of the plant. Economy in construction and other factors may indicate that the raising of that lower portion of the flow by means of pumps, to the desired plant elevation, is more desirable than lowering the plant structure. Some plants operate with this feature.

24. According to the above paragraph,

    A. a small percentage of the sewage reaches the plant by means of gravity
    B. all sewage reaches the plant by means of gravity
    C. where sewage cannot reach the plant by gravity, it is pumped
    D. pumping is used so that all sewage can reach the plant

25. According to the above paragraph, the reason that some plants are built above the level of the sewerage system is that

    A. these plants operate more efficiently this way
    B. gravity will naturally bring the sewage in at a lower level
    C. pumping of the sewage is more expensive
    D. these plants are cheaper to build this way

KEY (CORRECT ANSWERS)

1. D
2. A
3. A
4. B
5. C

6. D
7. C
8. C
9. D
10. B

11. C
12. D
13. A
14. D
15. B

16. D
17. A
18. A
19. B
20. D

21. A
22. D
23. B
24. B
25. D

ARITHMETICAL REASONING
EXAMINATION SECTION
TEST 1

DIRECTIONS: Each question or incomplete statement is followed by several suggested answers or completions. Select the one that BEST answers the question or completes the statement. *PRINT THE LETTER OF THE CORRECT ANSWER IN THE SPACE AT THE RIGHT.*

1.

   In the above sketch of a 3" pipeline, the distance X is MOST NEARLY _____ inches.

   A. 3 1/8 B. 3 1/2 C. 3 1/2 D. 3 5/8

2. The fraction 9/64 is MOST NEARLY equal to

   A. .1375 B. .1406 C. .1462 D. .1489

3. The sum of the following dimensions 1'2 3/16", 1'5 1/2", and 1'4 5/8" is

   A. 3'11 15/16" B. 4' 5/16"
   C. 4'11/16" D. 4'1 5/8"

4. The scale on a plumbing drawing is 1/8" = 1 foot.
   A horizontal line measuring 3 5/16" on the drawing would represent a length of _____ feet.

   A. 24.9 B. 26.5 C. 28.3 D. 30.2

5. Assume that a water meter reads 50,631 cubic feet and the previous reading was 39,842 cubic feet.
   If the charge for water is 23¢ per 100 cubic feet or any fraction thereof, the bill for the amount of water used since the previous meter reading will be

   A. $24.22 B. $24.38 C. $24.84 D. $24.95

6. At a certain premises, the water consumption was 4 percent higher in 2015 than it was in 2014.
   If the water consumption for 2015 was 9,740 cubic feet, then the water consumption for 2014 was MOST NEARLY _____ cubic feet.

   A. 9,320 B. 9,350 C. 9,365 D. 9,390

7. A pump delivers water at a constant rate of 40 gallons per minute.
   If there are 7.5 gallons to a cubic foot of water, the time it will take to fill a tank 6 feet x 5 feet x 4 feet is MOST NEARLY _____ minutes.

   A. 15   B. 22.5   C. 28.5   D. 30

8. The total weight, in pounds, of three lengths of 3" cast-iron pipe 7'6" long, weighing 14.5 pounds per foot, and four lengths of 4" cast-iron pipe each 5'0" long, weighing 13.0 pounds per foot, is MOST NEARLY

   A. 540   B. 585   C. 600   D. 665

9. The water pressure at the bottom of a column of water 34 feet high is 14.7 lbs./sq.in. The water pressure in lbs./sq.in. at the bottom of the column of water 12 feet high is MOST NEARLY

   A. 3   B. 5   C. 7   D. 9

10. The number of cubic yards of earth that would be removed when digging a trench 8 feet wide x 9 feet deep x 63 feet long is

    A. 56   B. 168   C. 314   D. 504

11. On test, a meter registered one cubic foot for each 1 1/3 cubic feet of water that passed through it.
    If the meter had a reading of 1,200 cubic feet, we may conclude that the CORRECT amount should be _____ cubic feet.

    A. 800   B. 900   C. 1,500   D. 1,600

12. A water use meter reads 87,463 cubic feet.
    If the previous reading was 17,377 cubic feet and the rate charged is 15 cents per 100 cubic feet, the bill for water use during this period is about

    A. $45.00   B. $65.00   C. $85.00   D. $105.00

13. Under proper conditions, the one of the following groups of pipes that gives the same flow in gals/min as one 6" diameter pipe is (neglect friction) _____ pipes of _____ diameter each.

    A. 3; 3"   B. 4; 3"   C. 2; 4"   D. 3; 4"

14. A roof tank is used to furnish the domestic water supply to a ten story building. This tank has a capacity of 5,900 gallons. At 10:00 A.M. one morning, the tank is half full.
    If water is being used at the rate of 50 gals/min, the pump which is used to fill the tank has a rated capacity of 90 gals/min, the time it would take to fill the tank under these conditions is MOST NEARLY _____ hour(s), _____ minutes.

    A. 2; 8   B. 1; 14   C. 2; 32   D. 1; 2

15. The number of gallons of water contained in a cylindrical swimming pool 8 feet in diameter and filled to a depth of 3 feet 6 inches is MOST NEARLY (assume 7.5 gallons = 1 cubic foot)

    A. 30   B. 225   C. 1,320   D. 3,000

16. The charge for metered water is 52 1/2 cents per hundred cubic feet, with a minimum charge of $21 per annum. Of the following, the SMALLEST water usage in hundred cubic feet that would result in a charge GREATER than the minimum is

    A. 39   B. 40   C. 41   D. 42

17. The annual frontage rent on a one-story building 40 ft. in length is $735.00. For each additional story, $52.50 per annum is added to the frontage rent. For demolition, the charge for wetting down is 3/8 of the annual frontage charge.
    The charge for wetting down a building six stories in height, with a 40 ft. frontage, is MOST NEARLY

    A. $369   B. $371   C. $372   D. $374

18. If the drawing of a piping layout is made to a scale of 1/4" equals one foot, then a 7'9" length of piping would be represented by a scaled length on the drawing of APPROXIMATELY _____ inches.

    A. 2   B. 7 3/4   C. 23 1/4   D. 31

19. A plumbing sketch is drawn to a scale of eighth-size. A line measuring 3" on the sketch would be equivalent to _____ feet.

    A. 2   B. 6   C. 12   D. 24

20. If 500 feet of pipe weighs 800 lbs., the number of pounds that 120 feet will weigh is MOST NEARLY

    A. 190   B. 210   C. 230   D. 240

21. If a trench is excavated 3'0" wide by 5'6" deep and 50 feet long, the total number of cubic yards of earth removed is MOST NEARLY

    A. 30   B. 90   C. 150   D. 825

22. Assume that a plumber earns $86,500 per year.
    If eighteen percent of his pay is deducted for taxes and social security, his net weekly pay will be APPROXIMATELY

    A. $1,326   B. $1,365   C. $1,436   D. $1,457.50

23. Assume that a plumbing installation is made up of the following fixtures and groups of fixtures: 12 bathroom groups each containing one W.C., one lavatory, and one bathtub with shower; 12 bathroom groups each containing one W.C., one lavatory, one bathtub, and one shower stall; 24 combination kitchen fixtures; 4 floor drains; 6 slop sinks without flushing rim; and 2 shower stalls (or shower bath).
    The total number of fixtures for the above plumbing installation is MOST NEARLY

    A. 60   B. 95   C. 120   D. 210

24. A triangular opening in a wall forms a 30-60 degree right triangle.
    If the longest side measures 12'0", then the shortest side will measure

    A. 3'0"   B. 4'0"   C. 6'0"   D. 8'0"

4 (#1)

25. You are directed to cut 4 pieces of pipe, one each of the following length: 2'6 1/4", 3'9 3/8", 4'7 5/8", and 5'8 7/8".
The total length of these 4 pieces is

    A. 15'7 1/4"   B. 15'9 3/8"   C. 16'5 7/8"   D. 16'8 1/8"

25.___

KEY (CORRECT ANSWERS)

1. A
2. B
3. B
4. B
5. C

6. C
7. B
8. B
9. B
10. B

11. D
12. D
13. B
14. B
15. C

16. C
17. D
18. A
19. A
20. A

21. A
22. B
23. C
24. C
25. D

SOLUTIONS TO PROBLEMS

1. 8'3 1/2" + x + x = 8'9 3/4" Then, 2x = 6 1/4", so x = 3 1/8"

2. 9/64 = .140625 = .1406

3. 1'2 3/16" + 1'5 1/2" +1'4 5/8" = 3'11 21/16" = 4'5/16"

4. 3 5/16" ÷ 1/8" =53/16 x 8/1 = 26.5. Then, (26.5)(1 ft.) = 26.5 feet

5. 50,631 - 39,842 = 10,789; 10,789 ÷ 100 = 107.89
   Since the cost is .23 per 100 cubic feet or any fraction thereof, the cost will be
   (.23)(107) + .23 = $24.84

6. 9740 ÷ 1.04 = 9365 cu.ft.

7. 40 ÷ 7.5 = 5 1/3 cu.ft. of water per minute. The volume = (6)(5)(4) = 120 cu.ft. Thus, the number of minutes needed to fill the tank is 120 ÷ 5 1/3 = 22.5

8. 3" pipe: 3 x 7'6" = 22 1/2' x 14.5 lbs. = 326.25
   4" pipe: 4 x 5' = 20' x 13 lbs. = 260
   326.25 + 260 = 586.25 (most nearly 585)

9. Let x = pressure. Then, 34/12 = 14.7/x. So, 34x = 176.4
   Solving, x ≈ 5 lbs./sq.in.

10. (8)(9)(63) = 4536 cu.ft. Since 1 cu.yd. = 27 cu.ft., 4536 cu.ft. is equivalent to 168 cu.yds.

11. Let x = correct amount. Then, $\dfrac{1}{1200} = \dfrac{1\frac{1}{3}}{x}$. Solving, x = 1600

12. 87,463 - 17,377 = 70,086; and 70,086 ÷ 100 = 700.86 ≈ 700 Then, (700)(.15) = $105.00

13. Cross-sectional area of a 6" diameter pipe = $(\pi)(3")^2 = 9\pi$ sq. in. Note that the combined cross-sectional areas of four 3" diameter pipes = $(4)(\pi)(1.5")^2 = 9\pi$ sq. in.

14. 90 - 50 = 40 gals/min. Then, 2950 ÷ 40 = 73.75 min. ≈ 1 hr. 14 min.

15. Volume = $(\pi)(4)^2(3\ 1/2) = 56\pi$ cu.ft. Then, $(56\pi)(7.5)$ = 1320 gals.

16. For 4100 cu.ft., the charge of (.525)(41) = $21,525 > $21

17. Rent = $73,500 + (5)($52.50) = $997,50. For demolition, the charge = (3/8)($997.50) $374

18. (1/4")(7.75) = 2"

19. (3")(8) = 24" = 2 ft.

6 (#1)

20. Let x = weight. Then, 500/800 = 120/x . Solving, x = 192 190 lbs.

21. (3')(5 1/2')(50') = 825 cu.ft. Then, 825 ÷ 27 ≈ 30 cu.yds.

22. Net pay = (.82)($86,500) = $70,930/yr. Weekly pay = $70,930 ÷ 52 ≈ $1365

23. (12x3) + (12x4) +24+4+6+2= 120

24. The shortest side = (1/2)(hypotenuse) = (1/2)(12') = 6'

25. 2'6 1/4" + 3'9 3/8" + 4'7 5/8" + 5'8 7/8 " = 14'30 17/8" = 16'8 1/8"

TEST 2

DIRECTIONS: Each question or incomplete statement is followed by several suggested answers or completions. Select the one that BEST answers the question or completes the statement. *PRINT THE LETTER OF THE CORRECT ANSWER IN THE SPACE AT THE RIGHT.*

1. The sum of the following pipe lengths, 15 5/8", 8 3/4", 30 5/16" and 20 1/2", is 1._____

    A. 77 1/8" B. 76 3/16" C. 75 3/16" D. 74 5/16"

2. If the outside diameter of a pipe is 6 inches and the wall thickness is 1/2 inch, the inside area of this pipe, in square inches, is MOST NEARLY 2._____

    A. 15.7 B. 17.3 C. 19.6 D. 23.8

3. Three lengths of pipe 1'10", 3'2 1/2", and 5'7 1/2", respectively, are to be cut from a pipe 14'0" long.
Allowing 1/8" for each pipe cut, the length of pipe remaining is 3._____

    A. 3'1 1/8" B. 3'2 1/2" C. 3'3 1/4" D. 3'3 5/8"

4. According to the building code, the MAXIMUM permitted surface temperature of combustible construction materials located near heating equipment is 76.5°C. (°F=(°Cx9/5)+32)
Maximum temperature Fahrenheit is MOST NEARLY 4._____

    A. 170° F B. 195° F C. 210° F D. 220° F

5. A pump discharges 7.5 gals/minutes.
In 2.5 hours the pump will discharge _____ gallons. 5._____

    A. 1125 B. 1875 C. 1950 D. 2200

6. A pipe with an outside diameter of 4" has a circumference of MOST NEARLY _____ inches. 6._____

    A. 8.05 B. 9.81 C. 12.57 D. 14.92

7. A piping sketch is drawn to a scale of 1/8" = 1 foot.
A vertical steam line measuring 3 1/2" on the sketch would have an ACTUAL length of _____ feet. 7._____

    A. 16 B. 22 C. 24 D. 28

8. A pipe having an inside diameter of 3.48 inches and a wall thickness of .18 inches will have an outside diameter of _____ inches. 8._____

    A. 3.84 B. 3.64 C. 3.57 D. 3.51

9. A rectangular steel bar having a volume of 30 cubic inches, a width of 2 inches, and a height of 3 inches will have a length of _____ inches. 9._____

    A. 12 B. 10 C. 8 D. 5

10. A pipe weighs 20.4 pounds per foot of length.
The total weight of eight pieces of this pipe with each piece 20 feet in length is MOST NEARLY _____ pounds. 10._____

    A. 460 B. 1,680 C. 2,420 D. 3,260

11. Assume that four pieces of pipe measuring 2'1 1/4", 4'2 3/4", 5'1 9/16", and 6'3 5/8", respectively, are cut with a saw from a pipe 20"0" long.
Allowing 1/16" waste for each cut, the length of the remaining pipe is

    A. 2'1 9/16"   B. 2'2 9/16"   C. 2'4 13/16"   D. 2'8 9/16"

12. If one cubic inch of steel weighs 0.28 pounds, the weight, in pounds, of a steel bar 1/2" x 6" x 2'0" long is MOST NEARLY

    A. 11   B. 16   C. 20   D. 24

13. If the circumference of a circle is equal to 31.416 inches, then its diameter, in inches, is equal to MOST NEARLY

    A. 8   B. 9   C. 10   D. 13

14. Assume that a steam fitter's helper receives a salary of $171.36 a day for 250 days is considered a full work year. If taxes, social security, hospitalization, and pension deducted from his salary amounts to 16 percent of his gross pay, then his net yearly salary will be MOST NEARLY

    A. $31,788   B. $35,982   C. $41,982   D. $42,840

15. If the outside diameter of a pipe is 14 inches and the wall thickness is 1/2 inch, then the inside area of the pipe, in square inches, is MOST NEARLY

    A. 125   B. 133   C. 143   D. 154

16. A steam leak in a pipe line allows steam to escape at a rate of 50,000 pounds each month.
Assuming that the cost of steam is $2.50 per 1,000 pounds, the TOTAL cost of wasted steam from this leak for a 12-month period would amount to

    A. $125   B. $300   C. $1,500   D. $3,000

17. If 250 feet of 4" pipe weighs 400 pounds, the weight of this pipe per linear foot is _____ pounds.

    A. 1.25   B. 1.50   C. 1.60   D. 1.75

18. A set of heating plan drawings is drawn to a scale of 1/4" = 1 foot.
If a length of pipe measures 4 5/8" on the drawing, the ACTUAL length of the pipe, in feet, is

    A. 16.3   B. 16.8   C. 17.5   D. 18.5

19. The TOTAL length of four pieces of pipe whose lengths are 3'4 1/2", 2'1 5/16", 4'9 3/8", and 2'3 1/4", respectively, is

    A. 11'5 7/16"   B. 11'6 7/16"
    C. 12'5 7/16"   D. 12'6 7/16"

20. Assume that a pipe trench is 3 feet wide, 3 feet deep, and 300 feet long.
If the unit cost of excavating the trench is $120 per cubic yard, the TOTAL cost of excavating the trench is

    A. $1,200   B. $12,000   C. $27,000   D. $36,000

21. The TOTAL length of four pieces of 1 1/2" galvanized steel pipe whose lengths are 7 ft. + 3 1/2 inches, 4 ft. + 2 1/4 inches, 6 ft. + 7 inches, and 8 ft. +5 1/8 inches is   21._____

    A. 26 feet + 5 7/8 inches   B. 25 ft. + 6 7/8 inches
    C. 25 feet + 4 1/4 inches   D. 25 ft. + 3 3/8 inches

22. A swimming pool is 25' wide by 75' long and has an average depth of 5'. 1 cubic foot contains 7.5 gallons of water. The capacity, when filled to the overflow, is _____ gallons.   22._____

    A. 9,375   B. 65,625   C. 69,005   D. 70,312

23. The sum of 3 1/4, 5 1/8, 2 1/2 , and 3 3/8 is   23._____

    A. 14   B. 14 1/8   C. 14 1/4   D. 14 3/8

24. Assume that it takes 6 men 8 days to do a particular job. If you have only 4 men available to do this job and they all work at the same speed, then the number of days it would take to complete the job would be   24._____

    A. 11   B. 12   C. 13   D. 14

25. The total length of four pieces of 2" O.D. pipe, whose lengths are 7'3 1/2", 4'2 3/16", 5'7 5/16", and 8'5 7/8", respectively, is MOST NEARLY   25._____

    A. 24'6 3/4"   B. 24'7 15/16"
    C. 25'5 13/16"   D. 25'6 7/8"

KEY (CORRECT ANSWERS)

1.	C	11.	B
2.	C	12.	C
3.	D	13.	C
4.	A	14.	B
5.	A	15.	B
6.	C	16.	C
7.	D	17.	C
8.	A	18.	D
9.	D	19.	D
10.	D	20.	B

21. A
22. D
23. C
24. B
25. D

SOLUTIONS TO PROBLEMS

1. 15 5/8" + 8 3/4" + 30 5/16" + 20 1/2" = 73 35/16" = 75 3/16"

2. Inside diameter = 6" - 1/2" - 1/2" = 5". Area = (π)(5/2")^2 ≈ 19.6 sq. in.

3. Pipe remaining = 14' - 1'10" - 3'2 1/2" - 5'7 1/2" - (3)(1/8") = 3'3 5/8"

4. 76.5 x 9/5 = 137.7 + 32 = 169.7

5. 7.5 x 150 = 1125

6. Radius = 2" Circumference = (2π)(2") ≈ 12.57"

7. 3 1/2" 1/8" = (7/2)(8/1) = 28 Then, (28)(1 ft.) = 28 feet

8. Outside diameter = 3.48" + .18" + .18" = 3.84"

9. 30 = (2)(3)(length). So, length = 5"

10. Total weight = (20.4)(8)(20) ≈ 3260 lbs.

11. 20' - 2'1 1/4" - 4'2 3/4" - 5'1 9/16" - 6'3 5/8" - (4)(1/16") = 2'2 9/16"

12. Weight = (.28)(1/2")(6")(24") = 20.16 ≈ 20 lbs.

13. Diameter = 31.416" ÷ π ≈ 10"

14. His net pay for 250 days = (.84)($171.36)(250) = $35,985.60 ≈ $35,928 (from answer key)

15. Inside diameter = 14" - 1/2" - 1/2" = 13". Area = (π)(13/2")^2 ≈ 133 sq.in

16. (50,000 lbs.)(12) = 600,000 lbs. per year. The cost would be ($2.50)(600) = $1500

17. 400 ÷ 250 = 1.60 pounds per linear foot

18. 4 5/8" ÷ 1/4" = 37/8 . 4/1 = 18.5 Then, (18.5)(1 ft.) = 18.5 feet

19. 3'4 1/2" + 2'1 5/16" + 4'9 3/8" + 2'3 1/4" = 11'17 23/16" = 12'6 7/16"

20. (3')(3')(300') = 2700 cu.ft., which is 2700 ÷ 27 = 100 cu.yds. Total cost = ($120)(100) = $12,000

21. 7'3 1/2" + 4'2 1/4" + 6'7" + 8'5 1/8" = 25'17 7/8" = 26'5 7/8"

22. (25)(75)(5) = 9375 cu.ft. Then, (9375)(7.5) ≈ 70,312 gals.

23. 3 1/4 + 5 1/8 + 2 1/2 + 3 3/8 = 13 10/8 = 14 1/4

24. (6)(8) = 48 man-days. Then, 48 ÷ 4 = 12 days

25. 7'3 1/2" + 4'2 3/16" + 5'7 5/16" + 8'5 7/8" = 24'17 30/16" = 25'6 7/8"

TEST 3

DIRECTIONS: Each question or incomplete statement is followed by several suggested answers or completions. Select the one that BEST answers the question or completes the statement. *PRINT THE LETTER OF THE CORRECT ANSWER IN THE SPACE AT THE RIGHT.*

1. The time required to pump 2,500 gallons of water out of a sump at the rate of 12 1/2 gallons per minutes would be _____ hour(s) _____ minutes.

    A. 1; 40   B. 2; 30   C. 3; 20   D. 6; 40

2. Copper tubing which has an inside diameter of 1 1/16" and a wall thickness of .095" has an outside diameter which is MOST NEARLY _____ inches.

    A. 1 5/32   B. 1 3/16   C. 1 7/32   D. 1 1/4

3. Assume that 90 gallons per minute flow through a certain 3-inch pipe which is tapped into a street main.
The amount of water which would flow through a 1-inch pipe tapped into the same street main is MOST NEARLY _____ gpm.

    A. 90   B. 45   C. 30   D. 10

4. The weight of a 6 foot length of 8-inch pipe which weighs 24.70 pounds per foot is _____ lbs.

    A. 148.2   B. 176.8   C. 197.6   D. 212.4

5. If a 4-inch pipe is directly coupled to a 2-inch pipe and 16 gallons per minute are flowing through the 4-inch pipe, then the flow through the 2-inch pipe will be _____ gallons per minute.

    A. 4   B. 8   C. 16   D. 32

6. If the water pressure at the bottom of a column of water 34 feet high is 14.7 pounds per square inch, the water pressure at the bottom of a column of water 18 feet high is MOST NEARLY _____ pounds per square inch.

    A. 8.0   B. 7.8   C. 7.6   D. 7.4

7. If there are 7 1/2 gallons in a cubic foot of water and if water flows from a hose at a constant rate of 4 gallons per minute, the time it should take to COMPLETELY fill a tank of 1,600 cubic feet capacity with water from that hose is _____ hours.

    A. 300   B. 150   C. 100   D. 50

8. Each of a group of fifteen water meter readers read an average of 62 water meters a day in a certain 5-day work week. A total of 5,115 meters are read by this group the following week.
The TOTAL number of meters read in the second week as compared to the first week shows a

    A. 10% increase   B. 15% increase
    C. 20% increase   D. 5% decrease

9. A certain water consumer used 5% more water in 1994 than he did in 1993. If his water consumption for 1994 was 8,375 cubic feet, the amount of water he consumed in 1993 was MOST NEARLY _____ cubic feet.

   A. 9,014 B. 8,816 C. 7,976 D. 6,776

10. Assume that a water meter reads 40,175 cubic feet and that the previous reading was 29,186 cubic feet.
    If the charge for water is 92 cents per 100 cubic feet or any fraction thereof, the bill for the amount of water used since the previous meter reading should be

    A. $100.28 B. $101.04 C. $101.08 D. $101.20

11. A leaking faucet caused a loss of 216 cubic feet of water in a 30-day month. If there are 7.5 gallons in a cubic foot of water, then the AVERAGE loss of water per hour for that month was _____ gallons.

    A. 2 1/4 B. 2 1/8 C. 2 D. 1 3/4

12. The fraction which is equal to .375 is

    A. 3/16 B. 5/32 C. 3/8 D. 5/12

13. A square backyard swimming pool, each side of which is 10 feet long, is filled to a depth of 3 1/2 feet.
    If there are 7 1/2 gallons in a cubic foot of water, the number of gallons of water in the pool is MOST NEARLY _____ gallons.

    A. 46.7 B. 100 C. 2,625 D. 3,500

14. When 1 5/8, 3 3/4, 6 1/3, and 9 1/2 are added, the resulting sum is

    A. 21 1/8 B. 21 1/6 C. 21 5/24 D. 21 1/4

15. When 946 1/2 is subtracted from 1,035 1/4, the result is

    A. 87 1/4 B. 87 3/4 C. 88 1/4 D. 88 3/4

16. When 39 is multiplied by 697, the result is

    A. 8,364 B. 26,283 C. 27,183 D. 28,003

17. When 16.074 is divided by .045, the result is

    A. 3.6 B. 35.7 C. 357.2 D. 3,572

18. To dig a trench 3'0" wide, 50'0" long, and 5'6" deep, the total number of cubic yards of earth to be removed is MOST NEARLY

    A. 30 B. 90 C. 140 D. 825

19. The TOTAL length of four pieces of 2" pipe, whose lengths are 7'3 1/2", 4'2 3/16", 5'7 5/16", and 8'5 7/8", respectively, is

    A. 24'6 3/4"
    C. 25'5 13/16"
    B. 24'7 15/16"
    D. 25'6 7/8"

20. A hot water line made of copper has a straight horizontal run of 150 feet and, when installed, is at a temperature of 45° F. In use, its temperature rises to 190° F.
If the coefficient of expansion for copper is 0.0000095" per foot per degree F, the TOTAL expansion, in inches, in the run of pipe is given by the product of 150 multiplied by 0.0000095 by

   A. 145
   B. 145 x 12
   C. 145 divided by 12
   D. 145 x 12 x 12

20.____

21. A water storage tank measures 5' long, 4' wide, and 6' deep and is filled to the 5 1/2' mark with water.
If one cubic foot of water weighs 62 pounds, the number of pounds of water required to COMPLETELY fill the tank is

   A. 7,440   B. 6,200   C. 1,240   D. 620

21.____

22. Assume that a pipe worker earns $83,125.00 per year.
If seventeen percent of his pay is deducted for taxes, social security, and pension, his net weekly pay will be APPROXIMATELY

   A. $1598.50   B. $1504.00   C. $1453.00   D. $1325.00

22.____

23. If eighteen feet of 4" cast iron pipe weighs approximately 390 pounds, the weight of this pipe per lineal foot will be MOST NEARLY _____ lbs.

   A. 19   B. 22   C. 23   D. 25

23.____

24. If it takes 3 men 11 days to dig a trench, the number of days it will take 5 men to dig the same trench, assuming all work is done at the same rate of speed, is MOST NEARLY

   A. 6 1/2   B. 7 3/4   C. 8 1/4   D. 8 3/4

24.____

25. If a trench is dug 6'0" deep, 2'6" wide, and 8'0" long, the area of the opening, in square feet, is MOST NEARLY

   A. 48   B. 32   C. 20   D. 15

25.____

KEY (CORRECT ANSWERS)

1. C
2. D
3. D
4. A
5. B

6. B
7. D
8. A
9. C
10. D

11. A
12. C
13. C
14. C
15. D

16. C
17. C
18. A
19. D
20. A

21. D
22. D
23. B
24. A
25. C

SOLUTIONS TO PROBLEMS

1. 2500 ÷ 12 1/2 = 200 min. = 3 hrs. 20 min.

2. 1 1/16" + .095" + .095" = 1.0625 + .095 + .095 = 1.2525" ≈ 1 1/4"

3. Cross-sectional areas for a 3-inch pipe and a 1-inch pipe are $(\pi)(1.5)^2$ and $(\pi)(.5)^2$ = 2.25π and $.25\pi$, respectively. Let x = amount of water flowing through the 1-inch pipe. Then, $\frac{90}{x} = \frac{2.25\pi}{.25\pi}$. Solving, x = 10 gals/min

4. (24.70)(6) = 148.2 lbs.

5. $\frac{4" \text{ pipe}}{16 \text{ gallons}} = \frac{2" \text{ pipe}}{x \text{ gallons}}$, 4x = 32, x = 8

6. Let x = pressure. Then, 34/18 = 14.7/x . Solving, x ≈ 7.8

7. (1600)(7.5) = 12,000 gallons. Then, 12,000 ÷ 4 = 3000 min. = 50 hours

8. (15)(62)(5) = 4650. Then, (5115-4650)/4650 = 10% increase

9. 8375 ÷ 1.05 ≈ 7976 cu.ft.

10. 40,175 - 29,186 = 10,989 cu.ft. Then, 10,989 100 = 109.89. Since .92 is charged for each 100 cu.ft. or fraction thereof, total cost = (.92)(110) = $101.20

11. (216)(7.5) = 1620 gallons. In 30 days, there are 720 hours. Thus, the average water loss per hour = 1620 ÷ 720 = 2 1/4 gallons.

12. .375 = 375/1000 = 3/8

13. Volume = (10)(10)(3 1/2) = 350 cu.ft. Then, (350)(7 1/2) = 2625 gallons

14. 1 5/8 + 3 3/4 + 6 1/3 + 9 1/2 = 19 53/24 = 21 5/24

15. 1035 1/4 - 946 1/2 = 88 3/4

16. (39)(697) = 27,183

17. 16.074 .045 = 357.2

18. (3')(50')(5 1/2') = 825 cu.ft. ≈ 30 cu.yds., since 1 cu.yd. = 27 cu.ft.

19. 7'3 1/2" + 4'2 3/16" + 5'7 5/16" + 8'5 7/8" = 24'17 30/16" = 25'6 7/8"

20. Total expansion = (150)(.0000095)(145)

21. Number of pounds needed = (5) (4)(6-5 1/2)(62) = 620

22. Net annual pay = ($83,125)(.83) ≈ $69000. Then, the net weekly pay = $69000 ÷ 52 ≈ $1325 (actually about $1327)

23. 390 lbs. ÷ 18 = 21.6 lbs. per linear foot

24. (3)(11) = 33 man-days. Then, 33 ÷ 5 = 6.6 ≈ 6 1/2 days

25. Area = (8')(2 1/2') = 20 sq.ft.

ARITHMETIC OF SEWAGE TREATMENT

The English system of measurements is used for computations at sewage treatment works, except in the case of a few determinations. The metric system will be mentioned where the metric units are used.

Basic Units

Linear	1 inch (in.)	= 2.540 centimeters (cm)
	1 foot (ft.)	= 12 inches (in.)
	1 yard (yd.)	= 3 feet (ft.)
	1 mile	= 5,280 feet
	1 meter (m)	= 39.37 in. = 3.281 ft.
		= 1.094 yd.
	1 meter	= 100 centimeters
Area	1 square foot (sq. ft.)	= 144 square inches (sq. in.)
	1 square yard (sq. yd.)	= 9 sq. ft.
	1 acre	= 43,560 sq. ft.
	1 square mile	= 640 acres
Volume	1 cubic foot	= 1728 cubic inches (cu. in.)
	1 cubic yard	= 27 cu. ft.
	1 cubic foot	= 7.48 gallons
	1 gallon (gal.)	= 231 cu. in.
	1 gallon	= 4 quarts (qt)
	1 gallon	= 3.785 liters (l)
	1 liter	= 1000 milliliters (ml)
Weight	1 pound (lb.)	= 16 ounces = 7000 grains
		= 453.6 grams
	1 ounce	= 28.35 grams (g)
	1 kilogram	= 1000 grams
	1 gram	= 1000 milligrams (mg)
	1 cu. ft. water	= 62.4 pounds
	1 gallon water	= 8.33 pounds
	1 liter water	= 1 kilogram
	1 milliliter water	= 1 gram

Definition of Terms

A *ratio* is the indicated division of two pure numbers. As such is indicates the relative magnitude of two quantities. The ratio of 2 to 3 is written 2/3.

A *pure* number is used without reference to any particular thing.

A *concrete* number applies to a particular thing and is the product of a pure number and a physical unit. 5 ft. means 5 times 1 ft. or 5 X (1 ft.).

Rate units are formed when one physical unit is divided by another.

$$\frac{60 \text{ ft.}}{2 \text{ sec.}} = 30 \frac{\text{(ft.)}}{\text{(sec.)}}$$

Physical units can be formed by multiplying two or more other physical units.

1 ft. X 1 ft. = 1 ft. X ft. = 1 ft.^{2} (square foot)

Physical units may cancel each other.

$$\frac{6 \text{ ft} \times 7.48 \text{ gallons}}{1 \text{ ft.}} = 6 \times 7.48 \text{ gallons}$$

Per cent means per 100 and is the numerator of a fraction whose denominator is always 100. It may be expressed by the symbol "%". The word *per* refers to a fraction whose numerator precedes *per* and whose denominator follows. Hence "per" means "divided by." It is often indicated by a sloping line as "/."

Problem: What is 15 per cent of 60?

$$60 \times \frac{15}{100} = \frac{900}{100} = 9$$

Problem: One pound of lime is stirred into one gallon of water.

What is the per cent of lime in the slurry?

$$\frac{1}{1+8.33} \times 100 = \frac{100}{1+8.33} = 10.7 \text{ per cent}$$

Formulas

Circumference of a circle = $\Pi D = 2\Pi R$

Area of a circle $= \Pi R^2 = \frac{\Pi D^2}{4}$

$\Pi = 3.1416$
Area of triangle = 1/2 base X altitude
Area of rectangle = base X altitude
Cylindrical area = circumference of base X length
Volume of cylinder = area of base X length
Volume of rectangular tank = area of bottom X depth
Volume of cone = 1/3 X area of base X height
Velocity = distance divided by time. Inches, feet, or miles divided by hours, minutes, or seconds.
Discharge = volume of flow divided by time.
  Gallons or cubic feet divided by days, hours, minutes, or seconds.
  1 cu. ft. per sec. = 647,000 gallons per day.
  1 mgd = 1.54 cfs = 92.4 cfm

Detention Time. The theoretical time equals the volume of tank divided by the flow per unit time. The flow volume and tank volume must be in the same units.

$$\frac{20{,}000 \text{ gal}}{200 \frac{\text{gal}}{\text{min.}}} = 100 \text{ minutes}$$

Problem: A tank is 60 X 20 X 30 ft. The flow is 5 mgd.

What is the detention time in hours?

1 mgd = 92.4 cfm

$$\frac{60 \text{ ft.} \times 20 \text{ ft.} \times 30 \text{ ft.}}{92.4 \times 5 \frac{\text{ft}^3}{\text{min}}} = 78 \text{ min. or 1 hr. and 18 min. or 1.3 hours}$$

Surface Settling Rate:

This means gallons per square foot of tank surface per day.

Problem: If the daily flow is 0.5 mgd and the tank is 50 ft. long and 12 ft. wide, calculate the surface settling rate.

$$\frac{500,000 \text{ gal./day}}{50 \text{ ft.} \times 12 \text{ ft.}} = \frac{833 \text{ gal.}}{\text{ft.}^2 \times \text{day}}$$

Weir Overflow Rate:

This means gallons per day per foot length of weir.

Problem: A circular settling tank is 90 ft. in diameter. The flow is 3.0 mgd. Calculate the weir overflow rate.

$$\frac{3,000,000 \text{ gal./day}}{\Pi \times 90 \text{ ft.}} = \frac{10,600 \text{ gal}}{\text{ft.} \times \text{day}}$$

Rate of Filtration: The mgd is divided by the acres of stone to give

$$\frac{\text{mg}}{\text{acre} \times \text{day}} = \text{mgad}$$

$$\frac{\text{mg}}{\text{acre} \times \text{ft.} \times \text{day}} = \text{mgaftd}$$

An acre-ft. is an acre in area and 1 ft. deep.
A fixed-nozzle filter is 140 x 125 feet. Stone is six feet deep. Flow is 9 mgd. Calculate the rate of dosing or hydraulic loading in mg per acre-foot per day.

$$\frac{140 \times 125}{43560} = \text{acres} = 0.402$$

$$0.402 \times 6 = 2.412 \text{ acre-feet}$$

$$\frac{9}{2.412} = \frac{\text{mg}}{\text{acre} \times \text{ft.} \times \text{day}} = 3.73$$

The BOD of a settling tank effluent is 200 ppm. If 15 lb. of BOD per 1000 ft.^{3} of stone is to be the organic loading, how many cubic feet of stone are necessary with a hydraulic loading of 3 mgd.

$$\frac{200 \times 8.33 \times 3 \times 1000}{15} = 333,333 \text{ ft.}^3$$

$$\frac{333,333}{6} = 55,500 \text{ ft.}^2 \text{ for filter area if stone is 6 ft. deep.}$$

Parts per million:

This is a weight ratio. Any unit may be used; pounds per million pounds or milligrams per liter if the liquid has a specific gravity equal to water or very nearly so. 1 liter of water = 1,000,000 milligrams.

1 ppm = 8.33 lbs. per million gallons
1 ppm = 1 milligram per liter

A sewage with 600 ppm suspended solids has 600 X 8.33 = 4998 lb. of suspended solids per million gallons.

Efficiency of Removal:

$$\frac{\text{ppm influent - ppm effueny}}{\text{ppm influent}} \cdot 100 = \text{percent efficiency of removal}$$

Percent of Moisture:

$$\frac{\text{wt. of wet sludge - wt. of day sludge}}{\text{wt. of wet sludge}} \cdot 100 = \text{percent moisture}$$

Percent of Dry solids:

$$\frac{\text{wt. of day sludge}}{\text{wt. of wet sludge}} \cdot 100 = \text{parcent day solids}$$

Other calculated quantities that need no special explanation are:
    Square feet of sludge drying bed per capita
    Cubic feet of digestion space per capita
    Cubic feet of sludge produced per day per capita
    Cubic feet of grit per million gallons
    Pounds of sludge per capita per day
    Cubic feet of gas per capita per day
    Kilowatt-hours per million gallons pumped

Specific Gravity: This is the ratio of the density of a substance to the density of water. There is no unit. Density = the weight of unit volume.

$$\text{S.G.} = \frac{(\text{wt. bottle with sludge}) - (\text{wt. of empty bottle})}{(\text{wt. bottle with water}) - (\text{wt. of empty bottle})}$$

1 gallon of water = 8.33 lbs.
1 cu. ft. of water = 62.4 lbs.
These vary slightly with temperature.
    Water at 32° F. = 62.417 lb./ft.^{3}

Water at 62° F. = 62.355 lb./ft.^{3}
Water at 212° F. = 59.7 lb./ft.^{3}
Ice = 57.5 lb./ft.^{3}

Problem: What is the weight of dry solids in 1000 gallons of 10% sludge whose specific gravity is 1.04?

$$1000 \times 8.33 \times 1.40 \times \frac{10}{100} = 866.3 \text{ lbs.}$$

Mixtures:

If two materials of different percentages are to be mixed to produce an intermediate percentage, it may be done by rectangle method. Problem: We have 30 per cent and 50 per cent material. In what ratio shall they be mixed to produce 37 per cent material.

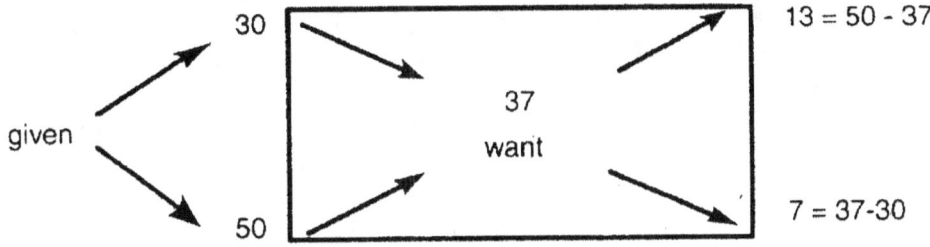

Desired ration is 13 parts of the 30 per cent and 7 parts of the 50 per cent. This will give us 20 parts of 37 per cent.

BASIC FUNDAMENTALS OF WATER QUALITY

TABLE OF CONTENTS

	Page
Reasons for Water Treatment	1
Quality Control Tests	2
Drinking Water Standards	3
Composition of Water from Various Sources	5
Self-Purification and Storage	8
Methods of Water Treatment	10

BASIC FUNDAMENTALS OF WATER QUALITY

Water, if strictly defined in the chemical sense, is H_2O a compound which, like all other pure substances, has a definite and constant composition. Therefore it should, like any pure compound, exhibit predictable chemical and physical characteristics. Indeed, the properties of a pure compound are so dependable that they may be used for identification if an unknown sample is submitted to a laboratory. In other words, water might be expected to be the same, regardless of its origin. In this context, discussing the "quality" of water, or of water from a particular source, would be rather meaningless.

One of the predictable physical properties of this widely distributed compound is a rather remarkable power to dissovle other materials. Familiar as we are with its characteristics, we tend to accept the solvent power of water as a matter of course, and to see nothing remarkable in it. But if water is compared with other known liquids, it is found that none of the others is capable of dissolving so wide a range of compounds of varying compositions. As a result, water seldom if very occurs in nature in a chemically pure state.

In addition to a variety of dissolved materials, water drawn from a natural source usually contains particles of insoluble, or at least undissolved, materials in suspension. The size and the concentration of these suspended particles vary considerably, depending upon the source, from the sand grains sometimes present in rapid, turbulent surface streams to the submicroscopic dispersions known as colloids. Included among the suspended particles, there may be living cells of thousands of different kinds of microorganisms.

Thus, when we speak of the quality of water, our concern is not really with the water itself, but with the other materials present. It is these impurities which determine, to a very large degree, the suitability of a water source for human uses, the problems associated with utilizing it, and the kind and extent of treatment required.

Reasons for Water Treatment

In the broadest possible terms, the objectives of water treatment may be classified under three general headings: (1) to protect the health of the community, (2) to supply a product which is esthetically desirable, and (3) to protect the property of the consumers. Each of these is so broad that it requires further explanation, and each embraces several specific methods of treatment.

Protection of the public health implies first that the treated water must be free of microorganisms capable of causing human disease, and second that the concentrations of any chemical substances which are poisonous or otherwise harmful must be reduced to safe levels. Only rarely do raw water supplies contain significant levels of toxic chemicals. But, more often than not, the microbiological quality of the water requires improvement or protection. In the United States, this aspect of water treatment has progressed to the point that the physiological safety of public water supplies usually is taken for granted. In some parts of the world, it is considered necessary when visiting a strange city to carry a private supply of drinking water, or to inquire whether it is safe to drink the local supply. The situation in the United States, which is unquestionably a credit to the water treatment profession, has permitted increased attention to the other two general objectives mentioned in the previous paragraph.

An esthetically desirable water supply requires that the final product shall be as low as possible in color, turbidity, and suspended solids, as cold as possible, and free from undesirable tastes and odors. Since the subject of tastes and odors is highly subjective, it may be impossible to produce a product which is equally pleasing to all consumers. However, strong, distinctive tastes and odors, as well as those which are disagreeable to a significant percentage of the population, are definitely to be avoided. The esthetic quality of a water supply cannot be completely divorced from the question of public health, since objections to the taste, odor, color, etc. of a perfectly safe public supply may prompt consumers to use water from another source which is more attractive, but which, due to lack of protection, may be considerably more dangerous.

The question of property protection is a broad one, and its specific implications depend upon the purpose for which the water is used. Thus the requirements may, and occasionally do, vary among different consumers using the same supply. For domestic supplies, the usual requirements are that the water shall not be excessively corrosive to plumbing and other metal equipment, that it shall not deposit troublesome quantities of scale, and that it shall not stain porcelain plumbing fixtures. For industrial purposes, the requirements may be even more stringent. For example, more than 10 ppm of chlorides interfere with the manufacture of insulating paper. Generally speaking, public suppliers do not find it practical to meet the strict and sometimes varied requirements of their industrial customers. Instead, they maintain a quality suitable for domestic consumption, and if necessary the industries provide further treatment on their own premises.

Quality Control Tests

In his efforts to maintain the quality of his product, the operator or superintendent of a water treatment plant relies upon various chemical and physical tests. In this way, he accomplishes several purposes. Most importantly, perhaps, he assures himself of his success in meeting the standards which are required and desired. If for any reason the quality temporarily becomes unsatisfactory, the test results advise him of the problem, and permit prompt corrective action. By keeping permanent records of the results, he is in a position to demonstrate the quality of his product to the regulatory authorities, or to any other interested individual or agency.

Tests used for monitoring or controlling water quality are suggested by the objectives listed in the previous section. Few, if any, plants find it necessary to perform all the tests discussed in this manual. Ordinarily, the only tests selected for frequent, regular performance are those pertinent to the quality problems experienced at a particular plant. Other tests may be run less frequently to periodically provide a more complete evaluation of the water quality. Samples of the raw water as well as the treated water are often analyzed, since the former may provide information which is necessary to the control of the treatment plant. In some types of treatment, it is desirable in addition to analyze samples collected at intermediate points. Many suppliers also find it advisable to test samples collected from various parts of the distribution system to assure that the water quality is as acceptable when it reaches the consumer as when it leaves the treatment plant.

Determinations of bacteriological quality are most often based upon measurements of the numbers of "coliform bacteria." Although this group of organisms is not known to cause human disease directly, its presence and survival is considered to indicate the potential presence of disease organisms (pathogens), and consequently the number of coliforms present is strictly regulated. In some plants, the enumeration of coliforms is supplemented by the "total plate count," which is an approximate measurement of the total microbial population of the water, or by determining the numbers of one particular species of the coliform group, *Escherichia coli*.

In the vast majority of plants, especially in the United States, control of the bacteriological quality of the water is accomplished by means of chlorination. Therefore, the determination of residual chlorine in its various forms becomes a most important analysis, even though it may not be rigorously correct to consider it a direct means of monitoring the water quality. Closely related to the measurement of residual chlorine is the determination of chlorine demand, which is currently defined as the difference between the concentration of chlorine added and the concentration remaining after a specified period of time. Measurement of the chlorine demand of the raw water is often essential to successful control of the bacteriological quality of the finished product, particularly if the chlorine demand of the source tends to be variable.

Tests for chemical substances known to be poisonous are not ordinarily conducted routinely unless there is reason to suspect the presence of one or more such materials. If the previous history of the water supply, or other circumstance, indicates the possibility of a problem of this kind, the analytical program should include measurement of the concentration of the offending substance, probably both before and after treatment. Otherwise, tests of this type might be included among those which are performed only periodically.

Among the tests related to the esthetic quality of the water, determinations of color, turbidity, suspended solids, and temperature are important. The measurement of taste and odor, unfortunately, is almost as subjective in the laboratory as in the consumer's home or place of business, notwithstanding various attempts to improve its quantitative aspects. For this reason, some plants, in which taste and odor problems are rare, seldom if ever perform the determinations routinely, but rely upon complaints to advise them of the occurrence of a problem. In other places, less fortunate, where strong or disagreeable tastes and odors are a frequent problem, such tests may be a regular part of the quality control program. In a few instances, specific substances such as sulfides and phenols, which are known to affect taste and odor may be measured. Likewise, the determination of iron and manganese may be included in this group, because excessive quantities of either may affect both taste and color. The measurement of dissolved oxygen is sometimes included too, since the majority of people seem to prefer the flavor of water in which the oxygen content is near saturation.

For domestic purposes, the analyses related to protection of property include those which reveal the tendency of the water to corrode metals or to deposit scale. The important tests in this group are those for pH, acidity, alkalinity, total hardness, and calcium. Sometimes a determination of conductivity and total solids may be included, and under certain circumstances a measurement of the concentration of sulfates is important.

Drinking Water Standards

The U. S. Department of Health, Education, and Welfare, through its agency, the U. S. Public Health Service, has published revised standards for the quality of drinking water. Although the federal Public Health Regulations govern only interstate carriers and certain other specified installations, their standards are widely used as guide by other regulatory agencies. Many of the latter have incorporated the PHS standards wholly or in part into their own rules.

Some of the provisions of the Public Health Service standards are summarized below. It must be noted, however, that the complete report[1] from which this information is abstracted includes a great deal of supplementary material which is important in the interpretation and application of the standards. Therefore, the figures quoted do not apply strictly nor without qualification in all cases.

The standard of bacteriological quality is based upon the number of coliform bacteria present. Detailed sampling and testing procedures are specified, and a complete and fairly elaborate description of the method of evaluation sets forth precisely what results are required of an acceptable supply. In effect, the number of coliform bacteria is limited to not more than one organism per 100 ml of water on the average, with not more than five per cent of the samples tested showing numbers greater than this limit.

In regard to physical properties, the turbidity should be less than five units, the color less than 15 units, and the threshold odor number less than three. If the turbidity standard is satisfied, the suspended solids will not be detectable.

"Recommended" limits of concentration established for a number of chemical substances appear in Table VII. These are not absolute standards. Rather it is suggested that these materials "should not be present in a water supply in excess of the listed concentrations where . . . other more suitable supplies are or can be made available."

TABLE I
RECOMMENDED CONCENTRATION LIMITS

Substance	Maximum Concentration, mg/l
Alkyl Benzene Sulfonate	0.5
Arsenic	0.01
Chloride	250.
Copper	1.
Carbon Chloroform Extract	0.2
Cyanide	0.01
Fluoride	0.8-1.7 (See PHS Standards)
Iron	0.3
Manganese	0.05
Nitrate	45.
Phenols	0.001
Sulfate	250.
Total Dissolved Solids	500.
Zinc	5.

In addition to the recommended standards which appear in Table I, concentration limits for certain constituents are established which may be considered absolute, in that exceeding any one of the limits listed provides grounds for rejecting the supply. These figures appear in Table II.

TABLE II
ABSOLUTE CONCENTRATION LIMITS

Substance	Maximum Concentration, mg/l
Arsenic	0.05
Barium	1.0
Cadmium	0.01
Chromium, Hexavalent	0.05
Cyanide	0.2
Fluoride	See Text
Lead	0.05
Selenium	0.01
Silver	0.05

For Fluoride, both the recommended and absolute limits are related to the climate of the locality in question. For the greatest part of New York State, the recommended optimum is 1.1 mg/l, the recommended upper limit is 1.5 mg/l and the absolute limit is 2.2 mg/l. For a small area in the northern part of the state, the corresponding limits are 1.2, 1.7 and 2.4 mg/l, and in the extreme southeastern part, 1.0, 1.3 and 2.0 mg/l.

Radioactivity is also limited, but the acceptability of a given supply is dependent to some extent upon exposure from other sources. A water supply is unconditionally acceptable in this respect if the content of Radium 226 is less than three micro-micro-curies per liter, the content of Strontium 90 is less than 10 micro-micro-curies per liter, and the gross beta-ray activity is less than one microcurie per liter. If the radioactivity of the water supply exceeds the values stated, then its acceptability is judged on the basis of consideration of other sources of radioactivity in the environment.

Composition of Water from Various Sources

As suggested before, virtually all the water used to supply human requirements has at some time, usually quite recently, fallen to the surface of the earth as rain or some other form of precipitation. At this stage, the quantity of foreign material it contains is likely to be at a minimum. Nevertheless, even rain water is not chemically pure H_2O. Not only does it dissolve the gases of the atmosphere as it falls, but it also collects dust and other solid materials suspended in the air. Since the atmospheric solids depend upon both the composition of the soil below and the materials released into the air from combustion, industrial processes, and other sources, analyses of rain or other forms of precipitation reveal surprising variations. In general, however, rainwater may be expected to be very soft, to be low in total solids and alkalinity, to have a pH value somewhat below neutrality, and to be quite corrosive to many metals. A "typical" analysis, subject to the variations mentioned above, might appear as follows:

Hardness	19	mg/l as $CaCO_3$
Calcium	16	mg/l as $CaCO_3$
Magnesium	3	mg/l as $CaCO_3$
Sodium	6	mg/l as Na
Ammonium	0.8	mg/l as N
Bicarbonate	12	mg/l as $CaCO_3$
Acidity	4	mg/l as $CaCO_3$
Chloride	9	mg/l as Cl
Sulfate	10	mg/l as SO_4
Nitrate	0.1	mg/l as N
pH	6.8	

After the water reaches the surface of the ground, it passes over soil and rock into lakes, streams, and reservoirs, or it percolates through the soil and rock into the ground water. In the process, a great variety of materials may be dissolved or taken into suspension. Consequently, it may be expected that the composition of both the surface waters and the ground water of a given area reflects the geology of the region, that is, the composition of the underlying rock formations and of the soils derived from them. In general, the presence of readily soluble formations near the surface, such as gypsum, rock salt, or the various forms of limestone, produce relatively marked effects upon the waters of the area. On the other hand, in the presence of less soluble formations, such as sandstone or granite, the composition of the water tends to remain more like that of rain. As one might expect, local variations are often considerable and occasionally extreme, both in the concentration of any one constituent and in the proportions of the various materials present. The examples given below should be considered with this in view. They are typical only in that they are not remarkable.

Surface water, in an area in which limestone is an important constituent of the geologic formations, might have a composition similar to the following:

Hardness	120	mg/l as $CaCO_3$
Calcium	80	mg/l as $CaCO_3$
Magnesium	40	mg/l as $CaCO_3$
Sodium & Potassium	19	mg/l as Na
Bicarbonate	106	mg/l as $CaCO_3$
Chloride	23	mg/l as Cl
Sulfate	38	mg/l as SO_4
Nitrate	0.4	mg/l as N
Iron	0.3	mg/l as Fe
Silica	18	mg/l as SiO_2
Carbon Dioxide	4	mg/l as $CaCO_3$
pH	7.8	

In such an area, the ground water often contains more hardness and bicarbonate than the surface waters. This is due in part to the longer period of contact with soil and rock, and in part to the fact that carbon dioxide, contributed by the decomposition of organic matter in the soil, greatly increases the solubility of some of the constituents. The folowing analysis might be considered typical of well or spring water in a limestone area:

Hardness	201	mg/l as $CaCO_3$
Calcium	142	mg/l as $CaCO_3$
Magnesium	59	mg/l as $CaCO_3$
Sodium & Potassium	20	mg/l as Na
Bicarbonate	143	mg/l as $CaCO_3$
Chloride	23	mg/l as Cl
Sulfate	59	mg/l as SO_4
Nitrate	0.06	mg/l as N
Iron	0.18	mg/l as Fe
Silica	12	mg/l as SiO_2
Carbon Dioxide	14	mg/l as $CaCO_3$
pH	7.4	

In areas in which the underlying formations are insoluble, that is, where they consist of sand, sandstone, clay, shale, or igneous rocks, the waters tend to he softer and more acid. In general, their content of most dissolved materials is lower. Acidity, however, may be higher than in hard water areas, since carbon dioxide picked up from the soil is not neutralized. Excepting in some areas of igneous rock, iron also tends to be higher in soft waters, since many of the iron compounds of soils and rocks are dissolved by the acidity of the waters. In many soft water areas, the differences between ground waters and surface waters are not as pronounced as in hard water regions, although many exceptions to this generality could be cited.

A more or less typical analysis of surface water in a region of generally insoluble soils and rocks follows:

Hardness	46	mg/l as $CaCO_3$
Calcium	30	mg/l as $CaCO_3$
Magnesium	16	mg/l as $CaCO_3$
Sodium & Potassium	9	mg/l as Na
Bicarbonate	42	mg/l as $CaCO_3$
Chloride	5	mg/l as Cl
Sulfate	12	mg/l as SO_4

Nitrate	1.5	mg/l as N
Iron	1.1	mg/l as Fe
Silica	30	mg/l as SiO_2

Ground water from a similar region might give analytical results similar to the following:

Hardness	61	mg/l as $CaCO_3$
Calcium	29	mg/l as $CaCO_3$
Magnesium	32	mg/l as $CaCO_3$
Sodium	26	mg/l as Na
Bicarbonate	60	mg/l as $CaCO_3$
Chloride	7	mg/l as Cl
Sulfate	17	mg/l as SO_4
Carbon Dioxide	59	mg/l as $CaCO_3$
PH	6.6	
Iron	1.8	mg/l as Fe

It is worth re-emphasizing that each of the constituents listed in the analyses above may vary over a wide range from place to place.

For example, waters are known with hardness values of less than 10 mg/l, and others have concentrations over 1,000 mg/l. Those quoted have been chosen to represent rather moderate, ordinary values occurring in two distinct types of situations common in the United States. It would be a mistake, however, to expect any water sample to correspond exactly to any one of the analyses given as examples.

Good Quality Water. Since waters from various sources may vary so markedly in composition, one may reasonably question which source should be considered most desirable. The problem has several practical consequences. For example, if a choice exists among several available sources, the final decision may rest upon judgment of their relative quality. Also, when the composition is modified by treatment, the objective is to approach, if not always to attain, the ideal.

The characteristics of "good quality water" are implied in earlier sections of this chapter, which discuss the objectives of water treatment and the standards formally adopted by the U.S. Public Health Service. Reviewing those sections will make it evident that the properties desired are mostly negative. That is, the objectives and standards are directed principally to avoiding undesirable qualities. The properties of " good" water may then be summarized in qualitative terms as follows:
1. Absence of harmful concentrations of poisonous chemical substances
2. Absence of the causative microorganisms and viruses of disease
3. Lowest possible levels of color, turbidity, suspended solids, odor, and taste
4. Lowest possible temperature
5. Minimum corrosivity to metals
6. Least possible tendency to deposit scale
7. Lowest possible content of staining materials, such as iron, manganese, and copper

This may appear to suggest that the ideal water contains the lowest possible quantity of total solids but this is not the case. Extremely soft waters tend to be excessively corrosive to metals, and many persons find them unpalatable. Moreover, they seem to be less effective in removing soap by rinsing than waters containing a little hardness.

Although there has been no formal recognition of a set of analytical values characterizing the "ideal" water, the following would probably be considered generally acceptable as an approximation:

Alkyl Benzene Sulfonate	less than 0.1 mg/l, preferably 0
Arsenic	less than 0.01 mg/l, preferably 0
Barium	less than 1 mg/l, preferably 0
Bicarbonate*	150 mg/l as $CaCO_3$
Cadium	less than 0.01 mg/l, preferably 0
Calcium*	70 mg/l as $CaCO_3$
Carbon Chloroform Extract	less than 0.2 mg/l, preferably 0
Carbon Dioxide*	6 mg/1 as $CaCO_3$
Chloride*	less than 250 mg/l, preferably 0
Chromium, Hexavalent	less than 0.05 mg/l, preferably 0
Coliform Bacteria	less than 1 per 100 ml
Color	less than 15 units, preferably 0
Copper	less than 1 mg/l, preferably 0
Cyanide	less than 0.01 mg/l, preferably 0
Fluoride	approximately 0.9 mg/l (somewhat dependent upon climate)
Hardness*	70 mg/l as $CaCO_3$
Iron	less than 0.1 mg/l, preferably 0
Lead	less than 0.05 mg/l, preferably 0
Magnesium*	preferably 0
Manganese	less than 0.02 mg/l, preferably 0
Nitrate	less than 10 mg/l, preferably 0
pH*	7.8
Phenols	less than 0.001 mg/l, preferably 0
Selenium	less than 0.01 mg/l, preferably 0
Silver	less than 0.05 mg/l, preferably 0
Sodium & Potassium*	37 mg/l as Na
Sulfate*	less than 250 mg/l, preferably 0
Suspended Solids	not detectable
Temperature	33 to 40 degrees Fahrenheit
Threshold Odor Number	less than 3, preferably 0
Total Dissolved Solids	less than 500 mg/l
Turbidity	less than 5 units, preferably 0
Zinc	less than 5 mg/l, preferably 0

*The relationships among calcium, bicarbonate, carbon dioxide, and pH should be such as to minimize scaling and corrosion. In some cases, these concentrations may dictate the most desirable concentrations of sulfate, chloride, magnesium, sodium, and potassium.

Self-Purification and Storage

Nature provides some degree of self-purification for all water that has been polluted or contaminated by the introduction of wastes, whether they originate as domestic sewage, industrial wastes, or drainage from yards, streets, and agricultural areas. The rate at which process occurs depends upon the nature and amount of polluting material as well as the physical, chemical, and biological conditions and characteristics of the water itself. Erroneous ideas are prevalent, however, particularly as to the value of aeration and its effect on flowing water. For instance, statements are sometimes made to the effect that "water will purify itself in flowing seven miles," or that natural aeration occurring at waterfalls and rapids will "oxidize" or kill bacteria. Actually, distance in itself has nothing whatever to do with self-purification in a flowing stream. Neither does aeration have much if any direct effect in killing bacteria. Time is the important factor, together wth proper conditions of temperature, sunlight, velocity of flow and many other complex chemical, physical, and biological characteristics. Quiescent sedimentation in a reservoir for a period of about a month may result generally in purification equivalent to that of filtration. Sluggish flow in a stream for a long distance may accomplish the same results.

The general appearance of a stream provides a useful guide to the degree of pollution. For instance, the bed of the unpolluted portion above sources of wastewaters usually is coated with a greenish brown deposit and green, rooted plants will thrive in protected areas. Just below a point of pollution, chemical and biological changes are evident, such as the gradual disappearance of the green plants. This stretch of the stream has been called the "zone of recent pollution."

Further downstream is the "zone of active decomposition", where the bed of the stream may have black sludge deposits, and a characteristic biological population adapted to a plentiful food supply but a limited oxygen supply. If the degree of pollution is great, the dissolved oxygen of the water may be completely exhausted. This results generally in objectionable conditions, the production of odors and gases, and a turbid gray or black appearance of the water. If, on the other hand, the degree of pollution is moderate and the dissolved oxygen content of the water is sufficient, odors are not produced. This condition results when the dissolved oxygen is replenished from the atmosphere and plant life at a rate faster than it is being used up in oxidation of the polluting material. The presence of rapids, falls, or even swiftly flowing water in this zone is helpful insofar as providing an adequate supply of atmospheric oxygen is concerned, since the rate of reaeration is closely related to the turbulence of the water. It should be noted, however, that a supply of oxygen exceeding the requirements does not accelerate the natural purification processes. Since the time is not shortened, a high flow velocity only means that the distance traveled before purification is complete is increased.

Eventually, unless additional pollution is discharged into the stream, the result is the production of an odorless, humus-like material in the stream bed. If the pollution contained nitrogenous materials, the concentration of nitrates in the water increases. There is restoration of the normal dissolved oxygen content, which favors the growth of green aquatic vegetation. Normal conditions are thus restored in this "zone of recovery," the length and position of which are dependent upon the degree of pollution and the natural conditions outlined above.

Essentially, the same action takes place in a natural lake or in an impounding reservoir, although the "zones" described above may not exist as distinct regions. This is due to the complications which are caused by the lack of currents with definite direction. Furthermore, a considerable amount of vertical mixing may occur due to variations in the density of the water. The changes of density, in turn, are caused by the differences of temperature of the water at the various levels in the lake or reservoir. The vertical mixing takes place continuously, but is most noticeable in the spring and fall when temperature changes are most rapid and mixing consequently most vigorous throughout the entire depth of the water. Very often this "turnover" of a lake or reservoir results in the occurrence of tastes and odors in the water supply, which may be due to changes in the types and numbers of microorganisms present, or to changes in the chemical and physical quality of the water.

In general, self-purification results in the removal of organic matter and the degree depends upon the dilution, the effectiveness of reaeration, sedimentation, and most important, the time interval available for biochemical action. The destruction of bacteria introduced with sewage, however, is controlled by a different set of factors. The rate is controlled by the water temperature, available food supply, the germicidal effect of sunlight, sedimentation, and the consumption of the bacteria as food by protozoa. This action is usually slower than the destruction of organic matter. Hence, bacterial contamination may persist long after the visible evidence of pollution has disappeared. Therefore, the only possible way of determining the influence of storage or of passage along a stream upon the bacteriological quality of the water is to measure bacterial numbers in representative samples of water collected at appropriate points.

Unfortunately, the effects of storage and time are not all beneficial in relation to certain characteristics of water. The results of biochemical purification are, for example, conductive to the growth of algae and other forms of microscopic plant and animal life. Although these organisms may have little if any effect on the health of a community as a result of drinking the water, they are the most common cause of tastes and odors, and generally, additional treatment is needed when they are present.

Methods of Water Treatment

The methods employed in the treatment of water depend, to a large extent, on the purpose for which the supply is to be used and the quality of the water being treated. For domestic use, it is desirable to remove any materials, either in suspension or in solution, which are detrimental to the appearance and esthetic appeal of the water. It is absolutely necessary to remove or kill any detrimental microorganisms, and to remove harmful chemical substances. On the other hand, industrial requirements for water quality vary, depending upon the use. For example, for stream generation the control of scale formation is of paramount importance, while textile mills and paper mills demand freedom from iron and manganese.

In general, the many methods normally employed in water treatment practice usually have as their main objective the reduction of the total quantity of foreign substances in the water. Even when the treatment process involves the addition of certain materials, the end result is usually the removal of more material than has been added. There are cases, however, in which certain constituents are removed by substituting other substances, and in some circumstances the content of certain substances may be increased deliberately, in order to impart certain desirable characteristics to the water.

Sedimentation. Sedimentation is more or less effective in the removal of suspended matter, depending upon the size and the density of the particles to be removed, and the time available for the process. Large or heavy particles are removed in a relatively short time, while a much longer period is required for light or finely divided materials. Some of the very finest such as eroded clay may not be removed even by several days' sedimentation. If the concentration of such "non-settleable" particles is excessive, then sedimentation alone is not an adequate method of treatment, and other means must be employed.

Coagulation. This is the technique of treating the water with certain chemicals for the purpose of collecting non-settleable particles into larger or heavier aggregates which are more readily removed. The resulting clumps of solid material, termed "floc," are removed by sedimentation, filtration, or both.

Filtration. Filtration of the water through sand, anthracite, diatomite, and other fine-grained materials is also capable of removing particulate matter too light or too finely divided to be removed by sedimentation. Filters often follow sedimentation units, so that the larger quantity of relatively coarse material is removed by sedimentation, to avoid rapid clogging of the filters, which in turn remove the particles for which sedimentation is not effective. Fine screens or microstrainers are sometimes used prior to sand filtration.

Disinfection. This broad sense means destroying pathogenic organisms. In the practice of water treatment in the United States, it is usually accomplished by the application of chlorine or certain chlorine compounds. Although many other treatment processes mentioned also have some effect upon the microbial population of the water, disinfection is the only step which is intended specifically for control of the bacteriological quality.

Softening. The removal of the elements which contribute hardness to a water supply, primarily calcium and magnesium is called softening. Many water supplies do not require softening, and in some cases, even though the water is hard, softening is not practiced. When domestic supplies are softened, usually the *lime-soda process* or the *ion-exchange process* is used. In the first, chemicals are added to precipitate calcium as calcium carbonate, and if further softening is required, magnesium is precipitated as magnesium hydroxide. Usually, the process results in a reduction of the total quantity of dissolved solids in the water. In the ion-exchange process, calcium and magnesium salts are converted to sodium salts, and little change in the total dissolved solids results.

Aeration. This may be used for a variety of purposes. Since volatile substances are removed in the process to some extent, and these may include materials which affect the taste and odor of the water, aeration is sometimes employed in connection with taste and odor control. Excessive carbon dioxide can also be removed in this way, and the corrosive effect of some water can be reduced. The removal of carbon dioxide by aeration sometimes also reduces the dosages of chemicals required in subsequent treatment processes. Finally, by supplying dissolved oxygen, aeration is often helpful in the removal of iron.

Iron and manganese removal. Specific processes to remove iron and manganese are employed only in waters which contain sufficient concentrations of these substances to cause persistent problems. A number of different techniques exist, and the choice depends upon the concentration and the chemical nature of the iron and manganese present.

Taste and odor removal. Taste and odor are affected by many of the treatment processes which are employed primarily for other purposes, and therefore, like some other characteristics, do not require special processes for control unless rather unusual problems exist. Which one of the several available processes proves to be most successful depends upon the nature and the concentration of the offending substances. It has been mentioned that some odors are effectively removed by aeration. Others may require either adsorption or oxidation for efficient control.

Corrosion control. This is accomplished in some cases by the removal of excess carbon dioxide (e.g., by aeration). In other cases, alkalinity is added to the water in the form of an alkaline chemical such as sodium carbonate.

Fluoridation. The objective of this process is to attain a concentration of fluoride in the water which imparts to the population the maximum degree of resistance to tooth decay.

CHEMISTRY

A knowledge of chemistry is desirable for all treatment processes, first to control the processes occurring in their plants and, second, to measure the effectiveness of such treatment as is used.

Chemistry, in its broad sense, deals with the composition of matter and how it changes. A description of matter should include a statement telling of what it is made and the manner or state in which it exists. Thus a description of water should state that it is composed of hydrogen and oxygen in certain proportions and exists as a liquid. Ice also is composed of hydrogen and oxygen in the same proportions, but exists as a solid. Such a change in matter is called a physical change and takes place when its manner or physical state of existence is changed but its chemical composition remains unaltered.

A *chemical change* is an alteration of the composition of matter, as that which takes place when quick lime is slaked to form hydrated lime or when iron rusts.

Actions or measurements relating to physical changes, such as temperature, rates of settling, particle size, velocity of flow, etc., are dealt with under the science of physics. Chemistry deals with the composition and change in composition of matter. It may be subdivided into two branches. Analytical chemistry deals with the breaking down of matter into its fundamental components. Synthetic chemistry is concerned with the building up of matter from its elemental constituents. Years of investigations have shown that all matter is composed of combinations of one or more fundamental substances called elements.

Elements are substances which cannot be subdivided into simpler sub-substances by ordinary chemical change. Water can be broken down into hydrogen and oxygen, but it has not been possible to break down hydrogen or oxygen to produce simpler substances. Therefore, hydrogen and oxygen are elements. In all, there are 102 stable elements, of which less than twenty are of importance to the chemistry of sewage treatment. A partial list of chemical elements is shown in Table 11. Elements themselves are made up of unit particles called atoms.

Atoms are the smallest pieces of an element that can take part in a chemical change. You might consider atoms as extremely small building blocks, each one of any single element being chemically the same, but different from atoms of other elements.

Isotopes are elements that may contain two or more distinct kinds of atoms, identical in their general chemical properties but differing essentially in mass. Most of the ordinary elements consist of mixtures of isotopes. Thus, chlorine consists of a mixture of two isotopes of mass 35 and of mass 37 in such proportion that the average atomic weight is 35.46.

TABLE 11
Basic Data for Elements and Radicals Encountered in Sewage Treatment (only the most common valences shown).

	Atomic Symbol	Atomic Weight	Valence	Combining Weight
Elements				
Aluminum	Al	26.98	+3	8.99
Calcium	Ca	40.08	+2	20.04
Carbon	C	12.01	+4	3.00
Chlorine	Cl	35.46	-1	35.46
Copper	Cu	63.54	+2	31.77
Hydrogen	H	1.008	+1	1.008
Iodine	I	126.91	-1	126.91
Iron	Fe	55.85	+3	18.62
Magnesium	Mg	24.32	+2	12.16
Manganese	Mn	54.93	Several	
Nitrogen	N	14.01	Several	
Oxygen	O	16.00	-2	8.00
Potassium	K	39.10	+1	39.10
Sodium	Na	23.00	+1	23.00
Sulfur	S	32.06	Several	
Radicals				
Hydroxyl	(OH)		-1	17.00
Nitrite	(NO_2)		-1	46.01
Nitrate	(NO_3)		1	62.01
Sulfate	(SO_4)		2	48.03
Carbonate	(CO_3)		2	30.00
Bicarbonate	(HCO_3)		1	61.01
Phosphate	(PO_4)		3	31.66
Silicate	(SiO_3)		2	38.05
Ammonium	(NH_4)		+1	17.03

Atoms of an element may combine with each other or with atoms of other elements to form molecules. *Molecules* are the smallest portions of a substance that can exist and still retain the composition of the substance. If two atoms of chlorine combine, we have a molecule of chlorine gas, which is how the free element chlorine exists in nature. If one atom of chlorine combines with one atom of sodium, a molecule of ordinary table salt is produced. When atoms of different elements combine, the product is called a compound and the smallest piece of a compound that can exist and retain the composition of the compound is a molecule. If we again consider atoms as building blocks and the blocks cannot be subdivided, it must follow that atoms of elements combine with atoms of other elements in steps of one atom at a time. Thus, one, two or three atoms of one element can combine with one, two or three atoms of another element, but never with a fraction of an atom.

Law of multiple proportions. This idea that matter is composed of combination of blocks, called atoms, explains the fact that elements can only combine with each other in certain definite proportions or multiples thereof. This immediately brings some order out of what might be chaos. One atom of carbon will combine with one atom of oxygen to form carbon monoxide. If one atom of carbon united with two atoms of oxygen, the product would not be the same. Actually, when one atom of carbon combines with two atoms of oxygen, an entirely different compound called carbon dioxide is formed. If we think of compounds as consisting of an aggregate of molecules each of which is made up of a definite proportion of atoms of different elements, then we can understand why a pure compound is always exactly the same in composition, regardless of how it is made or where it is found. Water, made by exploding hydrogen and oxygen, always is one part hydrogen by weight, and eight parts oxygen. Water made from burning gasoline is exactly the same. Water in Timbuktu, and water in the jelly you eat is all composed of one part hydrogen and eight parts oxygen by weight.

Atoms are extremely small particles which cannot be isolated and weighed. However, the weights of atoms of different elements can be compared and a relative weight obtained for each. As oxygen combines with many elements, it is convenient to consider it as a sort of standard for weight comparison and further, if a weight value of 16 is assigned to oxygen no element will have a combining weight less than one.

As molecules are composed of atoms, it must follow that the weight of a molecule is the sum of the weights of each atom that makes up the molecule.

Molecular weight is the sum of the atomic weights of the elements in the molecule. Thus, water is composed of 2 atoms of hydrogen, each of atomic weight 1.0 and one atom of oxygen, atomic weight 16, making the molecular weight of water $2 \times 1 + 16 = 18$. Similarly, carbon dioxide is one carbon atom 12, and two oxygen atoms each 16, making the molecular weight $12 + 2 \times 16 = 44$.

Names-The names of elements have been generally derived from Creek and Latin roots descriptive of their character. Thus, iodine is named from its violet color, chlorine from its green color, others from localities where they were discovered, and others are derived from the names of minerals from which they were extracted.

When only 'wo elements unite to form a compound, the name of the second element is modified to end in *ide*. Thus, when sodium and chlorine are combined to form a salt, it is called sodium chloride. Compounds of one element with oxygen are called oxides and when more than one oxygen atom is present, the Greek prefix *di* for two and *tri* for three is added. Thus, sulfur dioxide arid sulfur trioxide describe sulfur compounds containing two or three atoms of oxygen for each atom of sulfur.

Symbols. To illustrate chemical changes, symbols have been developed for the different elements which indicate one atom of the element. Thus, an atom of chlorine may be written as Cl and of oxygen as 0. Generally, the symbol is the first or first and second letter of the name of the element, although often the English name of the element is given but the abbreviation of the Latin or Greek name is used as the symbol. Thus, sodium is Na, the abbreviation of natrium, and iron is Fe, the abbreviation of ferrum. These symbols, together with the names of the common elements, are given in Table 10.

Formulae. By use of these symbols it is possible to write formulae which indicate the number and kinds of atoms making up a molecule. For example, HCl means that a molecule of hydrochloric acid is composed of one atom of hydrogen and one atom of chlorine. When more than one atom of an element occurs in a molecule, it is indicated by a number written under the symbol. Thus, H_2SO_4 means that a molecule of sulfuric acid contains two atoms of hydrogen, one of sulfur and four of oxygen. When a group of atoms is enclosed in parenthesis and a subscript number used, it means the whole group occurs in the moleule as many times as the value of the subscript numbers. For example: $Fe2(SO_4)_3$ means iron sulfate contains two atoms of iron and three sulfate groups each containing one atom of sulfur and four atoms of oxygen. This is done because certain elements combine to form groups which react with other elements in a manner similar to a single element. The group is called a radical and will be discussed more fully under solutions. See Table 10. Another type of group symbol is used to indicate the association of molecules of complex compounds with molecules of simpler compounds. The latter can enter into or be expelled from the complex molecule without themselves being changed. For example, aluminum sulfate is $Al_2(SO_4)_3$ but if prepared by cyrstallization from a water solution it will retain molecules of water and have the formula $Al_2(SO_4)_3 \cdot 18H_2O$, which is chemically like filter alum. This means that for every molecule of $Al_2(SO_4)_3$ present in the compound there are also eighteen molecules of water. However, if the compound is heated, the water as such can be expelled from the compound. Formulae of common chemicals with their common and chemical name are given in *Table 12* below.

Equations. By use of these formulae it is possible to write chemical changes graphically. Thus, $CaCO_3 + H_2SO_4 \rightarrow CaSO_4 + H_2CO_3$ means that when calcium carbonate and sulfuric acid react or combine, calcium sulfate and carbonic acid are formed. Similarly, when iron rusts it combines with oxygen to form iron oxide. This can be written $Fe + 3 O_2 \rightarrow 2Fe_2O_3$ However, one of the laws of chemistry is that matter can neither be created nor destroyed. Hence, in any chemical change there must be the same number of atoms in the substances produced as were present in the original compounds. Therefore, the above reaction must be "balanced" to produce an "equation" having an equal number of atoms on each side of the equation. Iron oxide, the product of the above reaction, contains two atoms of iron and three atoms of oxygen. To balance the equation there must be the same number of atoms of iron and oxygen reacting as exists in the product, Fe_2O_3. We might try to write the equation

$2Fe + 3O \rightarrow Fe_2O_3$, but this cannot be true because we know oxygen gas consists of two atoms or O_2. To make the equation conform to the facts, we then multiply everything by two.

Thus, $4Fe + 3 O_2 \rightarrow 2Fe_2O_3$, Now we have said that four atoms of iron react with three molecules of oxygen gas to produce two molecules of iron oxide, and the number of atoms on each side of the equation are equal.

TABLE 12

Common Name	Chemical Name	Formula
Ammonia gas	Ammonia	NH_3
Ammonia	Ammonium hydroxide	NH_4OH
Filter alum	Aluminum sulfate	$Al_2(SO_4)_3 \cdot 14H_2O$
Limestone	Calcium carbonate	$CaCO_3$
	Calcium bicarbonate	$Ca(HCO_3)_2$
Hydrated lime	Calcium hydroxide	$Ca(OH)_2$
Quick lime	Calcium oxide	CaO
	Chlorine	Cl_2
	Chlorine dioxide	ClO_2
Blue vitriol	Cupric sulfate	$CuSO_4 \cdot 5H_2O$
	Ferric chloride	$FeCl_3 \cdot 6H_2O$
Muriatic acid	Hydrochloric acid	HCl
	Sulfuric acid	H_2SO_4
Salt	Sodium chloride	$NaCl$
Soda ash	Sodium carbonate	Na_2CO_3
Soda	Sodium bicarbonate	$NaHCO_3$
Lye	Sodium hydroxide	$NaOH$
	Sodium phosphate	$Na_3PO_4 \cdot 12H_2O$
	Water	H_2O
	Hypochlorous acid	$HOCl$
Chloride of lime	Calcium oxychloride	$CaOC_2$
	Aluminum hydroxide	$Al(OH)_3$
Gypsum	Calcium sulfate	$CaSO_4$
	Carbon dioxide	CO_2
	Carbonic acid	H_2CO_3
	Monochloramine	NH_2Cl
	Dichloramine	$NHCl_2$
	Nitrogen trichloride	NO_3
	Methane	CH_4
	Calcium hypochlorite	$Ca(OCl)_2$

From Table 11 we find the atomic weight of iron is 55.85 and of oxygen is 16.0. Then, 4 atoms of iron are equivalent to 4 X 55.85 = 223.40. A molecule of oxygen equals two atoms or 2 X 16.0 = 32.0, the molecular weight. Three molecules equal 3 X 32.0 = 96.0. A molecule of iron oxide equals 2 X 55.85 = 111.70. the weight of two atoms of iron, plus 3 X 16.0 = 48.0, the weight of three atoms of oxygen, or a total of 159.70. Two molecules of iron oxide = 2 X 159.70 or 319.40.

The calculations would be:

$$4Fe + 3O_2 = 2Fe_2O_3$$
$$4 \times 55.85 + 6 \times 16.0 = 319.40$$

Now we can say that 223.40 parts of iron react with 96.0 parts of oxygen to produce 319.40 parts of iron rust, and they always will do so because the law of multiple proportion states that elements combine only in definite proportions. Suppose we had a piece of iron that had rusted and we wanted to know how much iron had been lost. If we carefully gathered and weighed all the rust and found it to be 79.84 grams, then we can calculate by proportion that 79.84 : 319.40 = ? : 223.40, so the weight of iron that rusted must have been

$$\frac{79.84 \times 223.40}{319.40} = 55.84 \text{ grams}$$

To illustrate how this is of value to a sewage treatment plant operator, let's suppose you wanted to know how much alkalinity was in the sewage you had to treat. It might be for control of a chemical precipitation processor possibly in connection with corrosion control. Suppose you have available a solution of sulfuric acid containing 2 mg H_2SO_4 in each ml. By titration, which will be explained in the laboratory, you find that 5.6 ml of the acid neutralizes all the alkalinity in a 100-ml sample of water. Calling alkalinity $CaCO_3$. the equation is H_2SO_4 + $CaCO_3$ $CaSO_4$ + H_2CO_3. From the atomic weights, we find that 98 parts of sulfuric acid react with 100 parts of calcium carbonate. We found that 5.6 ml of a solution of sulfuric acid containing 2 mg per ml reacted with the alkalinity in the sample. Thus, by proportions,

$$\frac{5.6 \times 2}{98} = \frac{X}{100} \text{ and we find } X = 11.5 \text{ mg } CaCO_3$$

Therefore, this weight of calcium carbonate must have been present in the 100 ml of sample. If we wish to express the concentration as parts per million, the answer would be 10 X 11.5 or 115 mg per liter of sample, which is equal to 115 ppm. Actually, in doing the test, the concentration of acid is adjusted so that the titration in ml multiplied by 10, if a 100-ml sample is used, gives the answer directly without any calculation.

Equations commonly used in water and sewage treatment are:

$$CH_4 + 2_2 \rightarrow CO_2 + 2H_2O$$

$$Cl_2 + H_2O \rightleftharpoons HCl + HOCl$$

$$Ca(OCl)_2 + Na_2CO_3 \rightleftharpoons 2NaOCl + CaCO_3$$

$$Al_2(SO_4)_3 + 3CaCO_3 + 3H_2O \rightleftharpoons 2Al(OH)_3 + 3CaSO_4 + 3CO_2$$

$$CO_2 + H_2O \rightleftharpoons H_2CO_3$$

$$CaCO3 + H_2CO_3 \rightleftharpoons Ca(HCO_3)_2$$

$$Ca(HCO_3)_2 + Ca(OH)_2 \rightleftharpoons 2CaCO_3 + 2H_2O$$

$$Ca(HCO_3)_2 + Na_2CO_3 \rightleftharpoons CaCO_3 + 2NaHCO_3$$

$$NH_3 + HOCl \rightleftharpoons NH_2Cl + H_2O$$

$$NH_2Cl + HOCl \rightleftharpoons NHCl_2 + H_2O$$

$$NHCl_2 + HOCl \rightleftharpoons NCl_3 + H_2O$$

$$CaCO_3 + H_2SO_4 \rightleftharpoons CaSO_4 + H_2CO_3$$

$$Ca(HCO_3)_2 + H_2SO_4 \rightleftharpoons CaSO_4 + 2H_2CO_3$$

Ionization. Somewhat different conditions prevail when chemicals are dissolved in water. You might consider that molecules of water enter between the atoms making up the molecules of the chemicals. The force that holds the atoms together is electrical. If they are separated by the molecules of water, each atom has an electrical charge. This splitting of the molecules, when dissolved in water, into charged atoms is called ionization. The charged atoms are called ions. Sodium chloride, when dissolved, ionizes into sodium ions and chloride ions.

$$NaCl \rightarrow Na^+ + Cl^-$$

The ions must he of equal and opposite charge or else the solution itself would have a charge, which is not true. When a salt such as ferric chloride ionizes, the ferric ion must have three positive charges to offset the negative charges of the three chlorine atoms.

$$FeCl_3 \rightarrow Fe^{+++} + 3Cl^-$$

Radicals. Under the heading Formulae, groups of atoms called radicals were discussed and it was said the groups reacted similarly to single elements. What was meant was that salts of the radicals ionize to form charged radicals instead of splitting into their component atoms. Thus, sodium sulfate ionizes to form sodium ions and sulfate ions and not charged sulfur or oxygen atoms.

$$Na_2SO_4 \rightarrow 2Na+ + SO_4$$
$$Fe_2(SO_4)^3 \rightleftarrows 2Fe^{+++} + 3SO_4^-$$

Not all compounds ionize to the same degree. Some in dilute solutions are very nearly completely changed to ions, others are so little ionized that for practical purposes they may be considered un-ionized. Others vary anywhere between the two extremes. Actually, the ionization of salts is a reversible reaction and at equilibrium, which is rapidly established, as many molecules of a salt ionize as ions combine to form molecules. The reaction then should be written.

$$Fe_2(SO_4)^3 \rightleftarrows 2FE^{+++} + 3(SO_4)^-$$

to indicate it is proceeding in both directions at the same time and at the same speed. It is well known that similar electrical charges repel each other and opposite charges attract each other. This explains why not all elements will react. If the electrical charges on the atoms are the same, no chemical reaction will take place. If the charges on the atoms are different, then combinations can generally be made to take place.

Acids. One of the characteristics of an acid is that it will ionize in water to produce positively charged hydrogen ions.

$$HCl \rightleftarrows H^+ + Cl^-$$

Not all acids ionize to the same degree. In dilute solution the "strong" acids such as hydrochloric, sulfuric and nitric acids ionize practically completely. This is why they are called "strong" acids, as the activity of an acid is determined by the degree of ionization. "Weak" acids only partially ionize. Thus, an equal amount of a "weak" acid would produce only a fraction of the amount of hydrogen ion that a "strong"" acid under similar conditions would produce.

Acids are also classified according to the number of hydrogen ions produced by one molecule of the acid.

$$\text{Example: Monoacid -HCl} \rightleftarrows H+ + Cl^-$$
$$\text{Diacid} - H_2SO_4 \rightleftarrows 2H+ + SO_4^-$$
$$\text{Triacid -}H_3PO_4 \rightleftarrows 3H+ + PO^-$$

Bases or alkalis are compounds which ionize in water to furnish hydroxyl ions (OH-). As with acids, bases ionize to different degrees.

"Strong" bases such as sodium hydroxide, and calcium hydroxide ionize to a high degree while "weak" bases only partially ionize.

Similar to acids, they are classified depending on whether one, two or three hydroxyl ions are produced by one molecule of base.

$$\text{Example:} \quad \text{Monobasic -NaOH} \rightleftharpoons OH^- + Na^+$$
$$\text{Diabasic -Ca(OH)}_2 \rightleftharpoons 2OH^- + Ca^{++}$$
$$\text{Tribasic -Al(OH)}_3 \rightleftharpoons 3OH^- + Al^{+++}$$

Equivalents. An equivalent weight of an acid is that weight of an acid which will furnish one molecular weight in grams of hydrogen ion. For monoacids, it equals the molecular weight of the acid in grams, for diacids it is half the molecular weight in grams, for triacids it is one-third of the molecular weight in grams.

Similarly, an equivalent of a base in the molecular weight in grams that will furnish one molecular weight of hydroxyl ions (17 grams). It is equal to the molecular weight divided by the number of hydroxyl radicals per molecule.

An equivalent weight of a salt is the molecular weight divided by the number of charges on the ions produced in solution.

pH value. Water ionizes to a slight degree to produce both hydrogen ion and hydroxyl ion.

$$H_2O \rightleftharpoons H^+ + OH^-$$

Thus, water might be considered both an acid and a base. Actually, because the concentration of both ions is the same, it is considered neutral. The concentration of both (H^+) and (OH^-) in pure water is 0.0000001 expressed in terms of gram ions per liter. Rather than use decimal figures for measuring hydrogen ion concentration, a pH scale has been adopted to record concentration in whole numbers.

The following has been prepared in which the concentration of hydrogen ions is expressed in values which are decimal multiples of ten.

Ionic concentration as Grams oj Hydrogen Ions (H^+) per Liter

of Solution		pH Value
1.0		0
0.1		1
0.01		2
0.001		3
0.0001		4
0.00001		5
0.000001		6
0.0000001	neutral	7
0.00000001		8
0.000000001		9
0.0000000001		10
0.00000000001		11
0.000000000001		12
0.0000000000001		13
0.00000000000001		14

The pH value is the number of places after the decimal point in the expression for the concentration of hydrogen ions per liter. It will be noticed that as the concentration of hydrogen ion decreases the pH value in the opposite column increases.

For reasons beyond the scope of this discussion, the number of (H^+) ions multiplied by the number of (OH^-) ions always gives the same value. That is. if the number of (H^+) ions is increased ten fold, then the number of (OH^-) ions will be automatically reduced to one tenth of what they were before.

$$(H^+) \times (OH^-) = k \text{ (a constant value)}$$

Because of this relationship, a scale of p(OH) values could be prepared in which the p(OH) value would always be that number which when added to the pH value would equal 14. That is. a solution having a pH of 3.0 would have a p(OH) of 11 and a pH of 9.0 would correspond to a p(OH) of 5.0. Because of this fact, a measurement of pH is also, indirectly, a measure of the OH" ion concentration and a second scale is therefore not necessary. pH values greater than 7.0 indicate alkaline characteristics.

Returning to the idea of "strong" and "weak" acids, if "strong" acids are highly ionized and produce a high concentration of hydrogen ion, then the pH value will be low. If an equivalent amount of "weak" acid produces less hydrogen ion, then the pH will be below 7.0 but not as low as in the "strong" acid solution.

Neutralization of acids and bases. Consider what happens when an acid solution and alkaline solution, each containing one equivalent of acid and base, are mixed:

$$HCl \rightleftarrows H^+ + Cl^-$$
$$NaOH \rightleftarrows OH^- + Na^+$$

The resulting solution would contain one equivalent of H^+, one equivalent of OH^-, plus the Na^+ and Cl^-. It was stated that water ionizes to H^+ and OH^- and their concentration from water is only 0.0000001 equivalents per liter. Thus, in the mixed solution the H^+ and OH^- would combine to produce water until the concentration of each was reduced from one equivalent of each to 0.0000001 equivalent of each.

$$H^+ + OH^- \rightleftarrows H_2O$$

In solution there would be left the $Na^+ + Cl^-$, which is what is obtained when NaCl is dissolved.

$$NaCl \rightleftarrows Na^+ + Cl^-$$

Both the acid and base would have disappeared. This mutual reaction of acids and bases is called neutralization. One equivalent of any acid will exactly neutralize one equivalent of any base with the production of a salt and water.

This is the basis of the determination of alkalinity in water. Under "Equations" it was shown how the alkalinity could be calculated if a solution containing a known amount of acid was used. However, if the acid solution is adjusted so that it contains a definite number of equivalents of acid, then one volume of the acid will neutralize an equal number of equivalents of base and no calculation is necessary.

Normal solution is one which contains one equivalent of acid or base per liter. Hence, equal volume of normal acids and bases exactly neutralize each other, or, if the acid is twice

the normality of the base, half the volume will be required to neutralize one volume of base,
ml X normality of acid = ml X normality of base

To determine alkalinity, a 1/50 normal acid solution is used to neutralize the alkalinity in 100 ml of sewage. If 5.6 ml of acid was required, then 5.6 (the ml of acid) multiplied by 1/50 (the normality of the acid) divided by 100 (the volume of the sample of sewage equals the normality of the sewage).

$$\frac{5.6 \times 0.02}{100} = \text{N of the sewage}$$

A normal solution of alkalinity equals the molecular weight of CaCO3 divided by 2 or 50 grams per liter. If the normality of the sewage as determined is multiplied by 50, the concentration of $CaCO_3$ in the sewage would be found in grams per liter. But the result desired is milligrams per liter, so that the grams per liter are multiplied by 1000 to change them into milligrams per liter or parts per million.

$$\frac{5.6 \times .02}{100} \times 50 \times 1000 = 56 \text{ppm}$$

It will be noticed that all the factors cancel, leaving the answer obtained by multiplying the milliliter of acid used by 10, if 100 ml sample is used, or 20 if a 50 ml sample is used. Thus, to actually do the test all that is necessary is to titrate 100 ml sample of sewage, measure the volume of acid used in milliliters and multiply this volume by ten to obtain the alkalinity in parts per million.

Acidity, alkalinity and pH. Acidity of water is a measure of the *total* amount of acid substances (H+) present in water expressed as parts per million of equivalent calcium carbonate. It has been shown that one equivalent of an acid (H+) equals one equivalent of a base (OH-). Therefore, it makes no difference whether the result is expressed as acid or base and for convenience acidity is reported as equivalnt of $CaCO_3$ because many times it is not known just what acids are present.

Alkalinity is a measure of the *total* amount of alkaline substances present in water and is expressed as parts per million of equivalent $CaCO_3$. Again this is done because the alkalis present might not be known but at least they are equivalent to the amount of $CaCO_3$ reported.

The activity of an acid or alkali is measured by the pH value. Thus, the more active the acid characteristics the lower will be the pH, or the more active the alkalis, the higher the pH will be. Alkalinity and pH are not the same, neither can be calculated from the other.

This can be illustrated as follows. If 1/1000 equivalent of a strong acid is added to 1 liter of water it will produce 1/1000 equivalent of H+. From the table on page 13 it is shown that 0.001 equivalents of H+ per liter equals pH 3.0. If 1/1000 equivalents of a weak acid, 10% ionized, is added to one liter of water, it will produce only one-tenth as much H+ or 0.001 X .1 = 0.0001 equivalents of H+ per liter and thus have a pH of 4.0. In both solutions the acidity or total amount of acid is the same, but one has a pH of 3.0 and the other 4.0. The one with the lower pH would more actively corrode iron than the one with the higher pH.

Organic Chemistry. The discussion so far has been concerned only with those compounds of mineral origin. There is another vast field of chemistry concerned with compounds of living matter or substances that had once been living matter. These are composed mainly of carbon, hydrogen and oxygen in many different proportions such as sugar, cellulose, or gasoline. Most of them do not ionize in water. Some, such as proteins, contain small amounts of nitrogen, sulfur and phosphorous. One characteristic of such compounds is that they volatilize on heating or burning, leaving no ash. The vegetable extract in natural water that causes the light yellow color similar to dilute tea is an organic compound. Algae, both dead and alive, are organic in nature, as is phenol, all of which cause taste and odor in water even in concentrations of only a few parts per billion instead of parts per million.

Most of the solid material suspended in sewage and a substantial part of the dissolved matter also is organic in nature. In fact sewage treatment is essentially a process for decomposing organic material into simpler chemical substances rapidly and under controlled conditions.

Solutions, Colloids and Suspensions. If small quantities of such common substances as salt, sugar or baking soda are added to water, the substances will disappear and the water will be just as clear as it was originally. Such a combination is called a solution and no chemical reaction has taken place between the dissolved substance, called the solute, and the dissolving liquid, called the solvent. The mixture may be thought of as molecules of the solute uniformly dispersed throughout the solvent such that there is no apparent interference with the passage of light through the solution.

On the other hand, if soil is mixed with water it will not disappear, but will prevent the passage of light through the water in proportion to the amount of the soil present. Such a mixture may be called a suspension and the permanency of the suspension is dependent on the coarseness and settleability of the soil particles.

If the soil contains very fine material, such as certain clays, some of it will remain uniformly dispersed throughout the water, but will still be visible and will diffuse a beam of light as it shines through. Such a mixture may be called a colloid or, as sometimes designated, a colloidal suspension.

The three terms, suspensions, colloids and solutions are thus used to differentiate progressively finer degrees of dispersion of substances in a liquid. The limit of the zones to which these terms apply is somewhat indefinite, arbitrary and beyond the scope of this chapter.

Colloidal suspensions are commonly found in sewage treatment. Raw sewage. Iinhoff tank effluent, the supernatant liquor from sludge digestion tanks all exhibit more or less turbidity which is colloidal in nature. The purification effected by trickling filter units is due in part to removal of colloidal material from the sewage by the jelly-like coating on the surface of the filter stones.

The Chemistry of Sewage Organic Matter. Most of the organic matter in domestic sewage consists of food scraps, fecal and urinary wastes from human bodies, vegetable matter, mineral and organic salts, and miscellaneous materials such as soap, synthetic detergents, etc. Some of these are solids, some are in solution, and some may be in colloidal suspension.

The food scraps are largely carbohydrates, proteins or fats. Fecal matter is made up of bits of undigested food, intestinal bacteria, and cellular waste from the body. Chemically it is probably largely body protein with some fats and considerable carbohydrates. The urinary wastes contain most of the nitrogen which is not retained in the body. This is in the form of ammonia or urea. Urea is a chemical compound which is easily decomposed to yield ammonia and carbon dioxide.

The vegetable matter in sewage is essentially garbage derived from kitchens of the community. Soaps, synthetic detergents, and mineral salts are, of course, waste products from domestic activities involving dish washing and laundering.

Saprophytic bacteria, always present in sewage, will decompose sewage organic matter, reducing the complex proteins, fats, and carbohydrates to simpler substances with production of simple gases such as carbon dioxide, hydrogen sulfide, methane, and ammonia and more complex substances such as organic acids, alcohols, etc. The course of the digestion and the resultant products are dependent to a large extent on the availability of oxygen. The products of digestion of sewage solids when oxygen is absent are quite different than the products of the digestion of the same material when oxygen is available. Digestion in the absence of free oxygen is called anaerobic digestion while that in the presence of free oxygen is called aerobic digestion.

Anaerobic digestion of sewage solids. The first stage of the digestion is characterized by the production of organic acids. Proteins, carbohydrates, and fats are decomposed by the anaerobic bacteria and the products of the decomposition are organic acids. This digestion stage is evident in sludge by a lowering of the pH and the presence of a disagreeable sour odor. Unless the amount of acid produced is excessive, the digestion will normally proceed to the second stage. With excess acidity, such as is obtained when the addition of fresh solids is too rapid, the bacteria will be destroyed and the process will end with the first stage.

The second stage is characterized by liquefaction of sewage solids under mildly acid conditions. The bacteria, by enzyme action, convert the insoluble solids material to the soluble form. This is in accordance with the requirements of the bacterial cells that all food material must be in solution before it can pass through the cell wall.

The third stage of digestion is characterized by production of gases. carbon dioxide, methane, and hydrogen sulfide; as well as an increase of pH and the production of carbonate salts.

The operator of a sewage plant can exert considerable control over the digestion process by taking steps to favor the orderly progression from one stage to another. In a properly operated sludge digestion tank, all three stages of digestion are progressing simultaneously but in different zones or layers within the tank. Physical and chemical tests for pH, the volume and identification of the gases produced, the relative amount of volatile material in the sludge solids and the drainability of the sludge when put on drying beds or on vacuum filters will reveal how well the process is going.

Aerobic digestion. In the aerobic digestion of sewage organic matter such as occurs in streams where the organic load is not excessive or on trickling filter units, the decomposition of the proteins, carbohydrates, and fats proceeds without the production of foul smelling organic acids and gases. The saprophytic bacteria have ample free oxygen available with which to accomplish the chemical transformations involved in decomposition of the complex compounds and the fixation of carbon, hydrogen, phosphorous, and sulfur elements into simple gases, relatively inert humus-like material, and mineral salts. Sewage plant operators are familiar with aerobic digestion which takes place in trickling filter units. The saprophytic bacteria are embedded in the gelatinous growth coating the stones, and humus material produced by the digestion periodically "unloads" from the filter and appears in the effluent.

The activated sludge process is another example of aerobic digestion of sewage organic matter. In this instance the consumption of free oxygen by the filamentous bacteria which are incorporated in the activated sludge is so rapid that extraordinary volumes of air are supplied by air compressors.

BASIC FUNDAMENTALS OF WATER CHEMISTRY

TABLE OF CONTENTS

	Page
Physical States of Matter	1
Chemical Change	1
Chemical Composition – Elements, Compounds and Atoms	1
Chemical Symbols, Formulae	3
Atomic Weight	3
Atomic Structure	4
Isotopes	5
Graphical Representation of Atomic Structure	5
Periodic Table of Elements	9
Valence and Atomic Structure	10
Valence and Chemical Combination—Valence Number	11
Laws of Chemistry	11
Molecules, Molecular Weight	12
Equations	12
Chemical Calculations	12
Ionization	14
Radicals	15
Equilibrium	15
Acids, Bases and Salts	15
pH Value	16
Equivalents of Acids and Bases	17
Neutralization of Acids and Bases	18
Indicators – Titration	18
Solutions	18
Organic Chemistry	21

BASIC FUNDAMENTALS OF WATER CHEMISTRY

Water treatment plant operators must have some knowledge of science, especially chemistry, to understand and control the water purification processes used in their plants. Fortunately a normal individual gains considerable knowledge of science during his lifetime. He observes material things and acquires through his personal experiences as well as through instruction by others a mass of information regarding their chemical and physical properties although he may not classify his knowledge on a scientific basis. The purpose of this chapter is to help a water plant operator to organize his present knowledge of chemistry and to add to it for the purpose of improving his understanding of water plant practices.

Physical States of Matter

All matter exists in one or more of three physical states: a) solid, b) liquid and c) gas. Some matter, water for example, can exist in all three physical states. Thus water may be solid (as ice), liquid (as ordinary water), or gas (as water vapor). Many times the transition from one physical state to another may be brought about by applying or taking away heat from the substance and this is true of water. It is not true of all matter, however, since an attempt to do so may have no appreciable effect or may bring about a different kind of change in the substance - a chemical change.

Chemical Change

Suppose we attempt to make a piece of wood become liquid by heating it, just as we can make a piece of ice liquid by heating it. We would soon find that heat does not liquify wood but chars it and, if enough heat is applied, burns it. We cannot by any means at our disposal restore the wood to its original state after it is burned as we could the original ice by refreezing the water. Excessive heat has produced a fundamental and irreversible change in the composition of the wood. This is an example of a chemical change—an alteration of both composition and properties of a substance.

Chemical Composition—Elements, Compounds and Atoms

Centuries of study have brought to man the knowledge that all of the many kinds of matter in this universe are composed of at least 114 basic substances which chemists call "elements." Some elements such as iron, copper, silver, gold and carbon, are well-known to everyone while others are so rare that they were isolated only recently after long years of effort. All materials are made of these elements existing alone or in combination as "chemical compounds."

Table I

Elements of Importance in Water Chemistry

Element	Chemical Symbol	Atomic Weight	Atomic Number	Valence Number	Corresponding Equivalent Weight
Aluminum	Al	26.98	13	3	8.99
Calcium	Ca	40.08	20	2	20.04
Carbon	C	12.01	6	2	6
				4	3
Chlorine	Cl	35.45	17	1	35.45
				3	11.82
				5	7.09
				7	5.06
Copper	Cu	63.54	29	1	63.54
				2	31.77
Fluorine	F	19.00	9	1	19.00
Hydrogen	H	1.008	1	1	1.008
Iron	Fe	55.85	26	2	27.93
				3	18.62
Magnesium	Mg	24.31	12	2	12.16
Manganese	Mn	54.99	25	2	27.49
				3	18.33
				4	13.75
				6	9.17
				7	7.86
Nitrogen	N	14.01	7	3	4.67
				5	2.80
Oxygen	O	16.00	8	2	8.00
Phosphorus	P	30.98	15	3	10.33
				5	6.20
Potassium	K	39.10	19	1	39.10
Silicon	Si	28.09	14	4	7.02
Sodium	Na	22.99	11	1	22.99
Sulfur	S	32.06	16	2	16.03
				4	8.02
				6	5.34

A chemical element may be defined as a chemical substance which cannot be decomposed into simpler substances by *ordinary* chemical change. Water, a chemical compound, may be decomposed easily into hydrogen and oxygen which are chemical elements. It is not possible, however, to decompose hydrogen and oxygen into still simpler substances without altering their basic identity. Table I lists a number of elements of particular importance to water chemistry and includes data regarding their properties. In the paragraphs that follow the significance of these data will be discussed.

The smallest part of an element which can exist and retain all of the chemical properties associated with the element is called an "atom." If one attempts to break down an atom of an element into lighter fragments, he may succeed if he applies extraordinary techniques, but after the breakdown, he no longer has the same element. He will have an element of lighter weight plus a considerable amount of energy in the form of heat and light. This process, popularly called "atom-smashing," or fission, is the basis for atomic energy and is outside the scope of this chapter.

Chemical Symbols, Formulae

It is convenient to represent each of the elements by a "symbol" rather than writing out its name. Symbols are in effect a form of shorthand applied to chemistry. (See Table I, column 2). Students of chemistry quickly learn the symbols for the more common elements and thereafter seldom write out their full names.

A combination of symbols to indicate a chemical compound is called the "formula" for the compound. A formula not only indicates the elements in the compound but by means of subscript numerals the number of atoms of each element in the compound.

Examples:
Symbol for hydrogen — H
Symbol for oxygen — O
Formula for water — H_2O; signifying that the compound, water, has 2 atoms of hydrogen combined with 1 atom of oxygen. Note that single atoms have no subscript.
Symbol for sodium — Na
Symbol for chlorine — Cl
Formula for sodium chloride (ordinary salt) — NaCl; signifying that the compound, sodium chloride, has **1** atom of sodium combined with 1 atom of chlorine.
Symbol for iron — Fe
Symbol for oxygen — O
Formula for ferric oxide (red rust) Fe_2O_3; signifying the compound, ferric oxide, has 2 atoms of iron combined with 3 atoms of oxygen.
Chemical formulas for other compounds of particular interest to water plant operators are listed in Table V (See page 73).

Atomic Weight

Elements, being material things have "mass," meaning that they are acted upon by the force of gravity. A practical measure of mass is "weight." In chemistry, the masses of all substances are expressed in terms of the metric system, the basic weight unit of which is the "gram." Different elements have different masses and this property together with other physical and chemical properties helps to identify elements.

Because of the different weight systems in effect in various countries of the world, the weights of elements are always stated in relative terms. The weight of an atom of carbon (the basic unit) is designated as 12 and the atomic weights of all of the other elements are designated by values which express the relationship of the mass of an atom of the element to the mass of an atom of carbon. On this basis, the mass of an atom of oxygen (atomic weight) is 16. This means, $\frac{\text{weight of an atom of oxygen}}{\text{weight of an atom of carbon}} = \frac{16}{12}$ The lighest element, hydrogen, has the atomic weight 1.008 and the heaviest, mendelevium (Md) has an atomic weight of 256. The heaviest naturally occurring element is uranium with an atomic weight of 238. Column 3 of Table I lists the atomic weights of the elements in column 1.

Formula weight — The formula weight of a compound equals the sum of the atomic weights of of all of the atoms making up the compound.

Atomic Structure

It is not necessary to have detailed knowledge of atomic structure to work with chemicals and make use of chemical reactions; chemistry was already an old science when various theories of atomic structure were evolved. Properties of chemical elements can be understood more fully and the mechanisms of chemical reactions can be explained more clearly through a knowledge of atomic structure. Some of the simpler concepts of this subject are presented here.

It was stated earlier that an atom is the smallest part of an element which can exist and still retain all of the properties of the element. Just how small is an atom? It is much too small to be seen with even the most powerful microscopes. It has been estimated that 100 million atoms would be required to make a line one inch long, and yet, despite the difficulty of studying such small objects, much has been learned about them. We know, for example, that atoms are composed of still smaller particles. These include protons, neutrons, electrons, and perhaps others. When they are associated together in a unit, namely an atom, they confer upon it characteristic properties. When by use of extraordinary force they are dissociated from each other the properties of the atom are altered.

We also know that the components of an atom are arranged in a fashion similar to our solar system with protons and neutrons representing the sun and electrons representing the planets. Just as planets orbit about the sun as a nucleus of the solar system, electrons orbit about the atomic nucleus of protons and neutrons. In our solar system each planet rotates in an orbit of its own but this is not necessarily true of atoms for one or more electrons may occupy a single orbit or "shell"—the term preferred by atomic scientists.

Let us now consider in greater detail the various components of an atom.

A proton is a particle of matter located in the nucleus of the atom. It has a mass of 1.007594 with respect to the chemical standard of mass carbon with a mass of 12.01. The proton carries a single positive electrical charge.

A neutron is also a nuclear particle. Its mass is 1.008986, only slightly heavier than a proton. It does not bear an electrical charge.

An electron is an extremely small particle which rotates in a shell about the nucleus. The mass of an electron is so small (0.000549) that it is usually ignored when considering the weight of an atom. It carries a single negative electrical charge.

For an atom to be electrically neutral it must have as many positively charged protons in the nucleus as there are negatively charged electrons in the shells surrounding the neucleus. Since the neutrons in the nucleus do not bear any charges their number does not affect the electrical polarity of the atom.

The most fundamental fact regarding an atom is that its identity is established by the number of protons in the nucleus. This is known as its "atomic number" (Column 4, Table I) and in a neutral atom it also represents the number of electrons in the shells outside the nucleus. If, by use of extraordinary methods, a proton is dislodged from the nucleus of an atom, the identity of the atom is changed, that is, the original atom disappears and a new atom of a lower atomic number and lower mass is created. In the process of splitting protons from an atomic nucleus (nuclear fission) a tremendous amount of energy is released and this is the basis for atomic energy which was brought to the attention of everyone in 1945 by the atomic bomb. The bomb represented a massive release of energy from fissionable material in the form of elemental uranium. Peaceful use of atomic energy involves the *controlled* release of energy through *controlled* nuclear fission, a much more difficult process than exploding a bomb.

Isotopes

Loss of an electron from an atom does not change its identity nor does the loss of a neutron. Loss of an electron merely imparts a positive charge on the atom and loss of a neutron produces an atom of the same identity but smaller mass than the original. Such an atom is known as an "isotope". Most atoms have isotopes and many have several. Oxygen, for example, has 4 isotopes O^{16}, O^{17}, O^{18}, and O^{19}. All of the forms of oxygen have 8 protons but 8, 9, 10, and 11 neutrons respectively. Atomic weights ascribed to various elements represent the average weights of their isotopes, taking into account their relative abundance in the natural state.

Graphical Representation of Atomic Structure

The spatial relationship of orbital electrons and the nucleus of an atom is complex and pictorial representations are often used in an attempt to make it more comprehensible to students. Since the atom with electrons is a 3 dimensional entity, a better picture of its structure can be obtained with 3 dimensional models. These are available for lecture purposes but, of course, cannot help with printed texts. Figures 1 through 13 may serve in some degree, however, to clarify the subject. In these illustrations the nucleus is represented by a circle, and protons and neutrons in the nucleus are represented by their commonly used symbols, "p" for proton and "n" for neutron. A numeral adjacent to each of these symbols represents the number of protons and neutrons respectively present in the nucleus. Electrons are represented by the symbol e and their orbital paths or shells are represented by larger circles.

A sharp observer on studying figures 1.13 will note two important features:
1. The first shell outside the nucleus has a minimum of 1 electron and a maximum of 2 electrons.
2. The second shell outside the nucleus, if its exists, has a minimum of 1 electron and a maximum of 8 electrons.

Because of space limitations, it is not possible to illustrate all of the rules of atomic structure although additional ones should be mentioned.

ATOMIC MODELS

FIG. 1

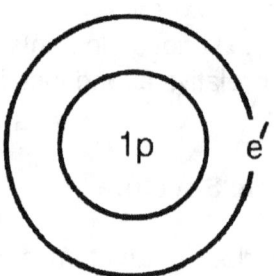

HYDROGEN (H)

FIG. 2

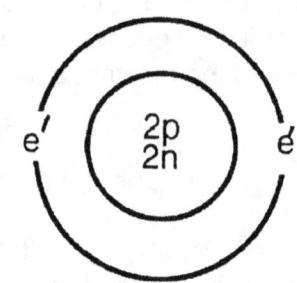

HELIUM (He)

FIG. 3

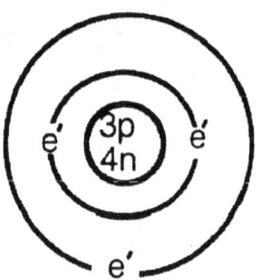

LITHIUM (Li)

FIG. 4

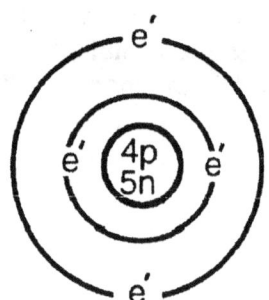

BERYLLIUM (Be)

FIG. 5

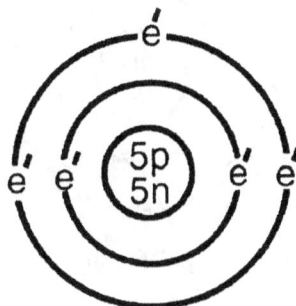

BORON (B)

FIG. 6

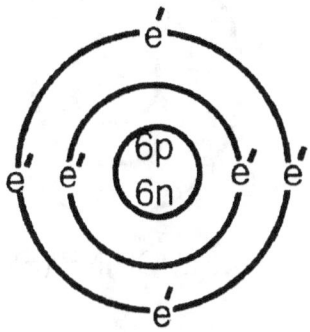

CARBON (C)

FIG. 7

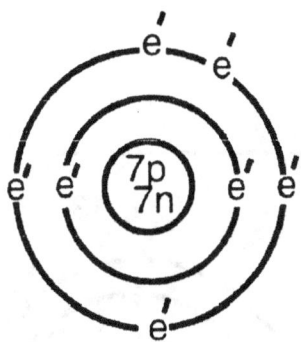

NITROGEN (N)

FIG. 8

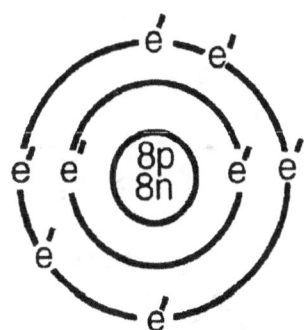

OXYGEN (O)

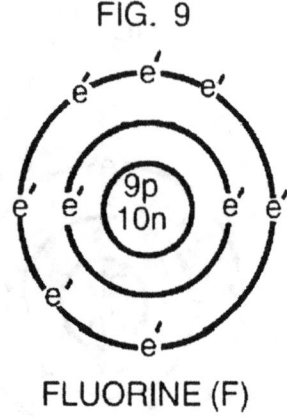

FIG. 9

FLUORINE (F)

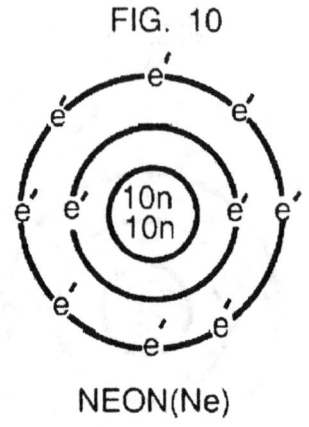

FIG. 10

NEON (Ne)

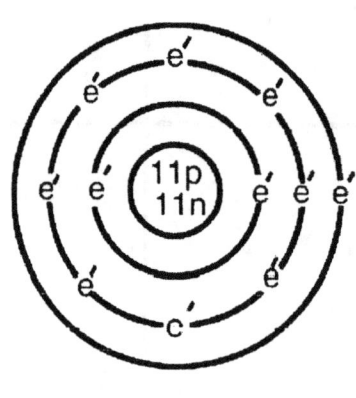

FIG. 11

SODIUM (Na)

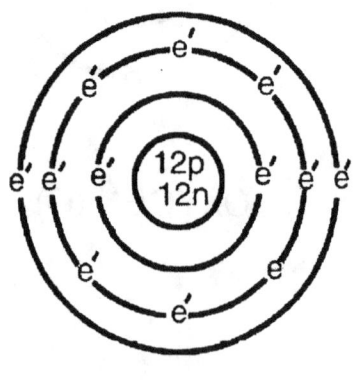

FIG. 12

MAGNESIUM (Mg)

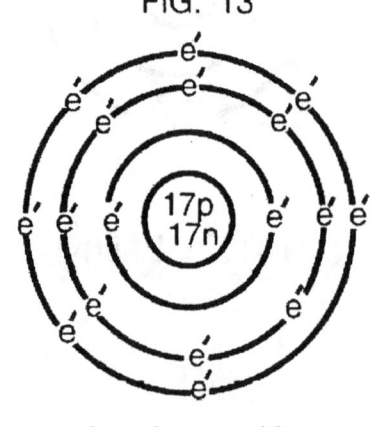

FIG. 13

CHLORINE (Cl)

3. The first 18 elements have electrons arranged in orderly progression whereby the first shell holds a maximum of 2, the second shell a maximum of 8 and the third shell a maximum of 8 and no new shell is started until the one preceding it is filled.
4. Beyond the 18th element, however, this orderly progression no longer prevails and elements with 2 or more unfilled shells are common.
5. The maximum number of electrons which can occupy a shell is dependent upon its position with respect to the nucleus and can be calculated by the formula:

$M = 2S^2$

Where M = maximum number of electrons in the shell
S = the number of the shell with respect to the nucleus.
6. There are never more 8 electrons in the outermost shell.

On the basis of these rules, four distinct types of elements are recognized:
A. Those which have atoms with no unfilled electron shells. These are inert elements which do not combine with other elements.
B. Those which have atoms with 1 unfilled shell. These are "simple" elements.
C. Those which have atoms with 2 unfilled shells. These are "transition" elements.
D. Those which have atoms with 3 unfilled shells. These are "rare earth" elements.

Periodic Table of the Elements

Mendelejeff, a 19th century Russian chemist, noticed what he called "periodicity" of physical and chemical properties of the elements and he devised a table in which he grouped the known elements according to their properties. He left places for elements not then discovered but which he expected would be discovered later on the basis of periodicity. The table published in 1872 was subjected to many adjustments and rearrangements but its original basis remains grouping of elements with similar properties. An illustration of the modern table appears in Fig. 14. Vertical columns represent "Groups" of elements arranged on the basis of the number of electrons in their outer shells. Elements in Groups I through VII have 1 unfilled shell and therefore are classified as "simple" elements. Group I elements have only 1 electron inthe outer shell, Group II have 2 electrons, ect. Group VIII elements have completed shells of 8 electrons and are therefore in the "inert" class. Inertness is quite evidently associated with the lack of space to add on electrons from other atoms.

"Transition" electrons having 2 unfilled shells are grouped near the center of the periodic table. These also are arranged on the basis of similarity of properties but the relationship is not so definite as for the simple elements.

"Rare earth" elements each having 3 unfilled shells are arranged in 2 series in a separate table below the main table.

The horizontal arrangement of the elements also has significance. All of the elements on a single horizontal level (a single period) have the same number of atomic shells. There are, therefore, 7 periods with elements having from 1 to 7 shells of electrons in their atomic structure.

The periodic table was of great help to early chemists in studying chemical properties of the elements and especially helpful in predicting properties of elements not isolated at that time. Students of chemistry still can learn much by study of the periodic table.

FIG 14

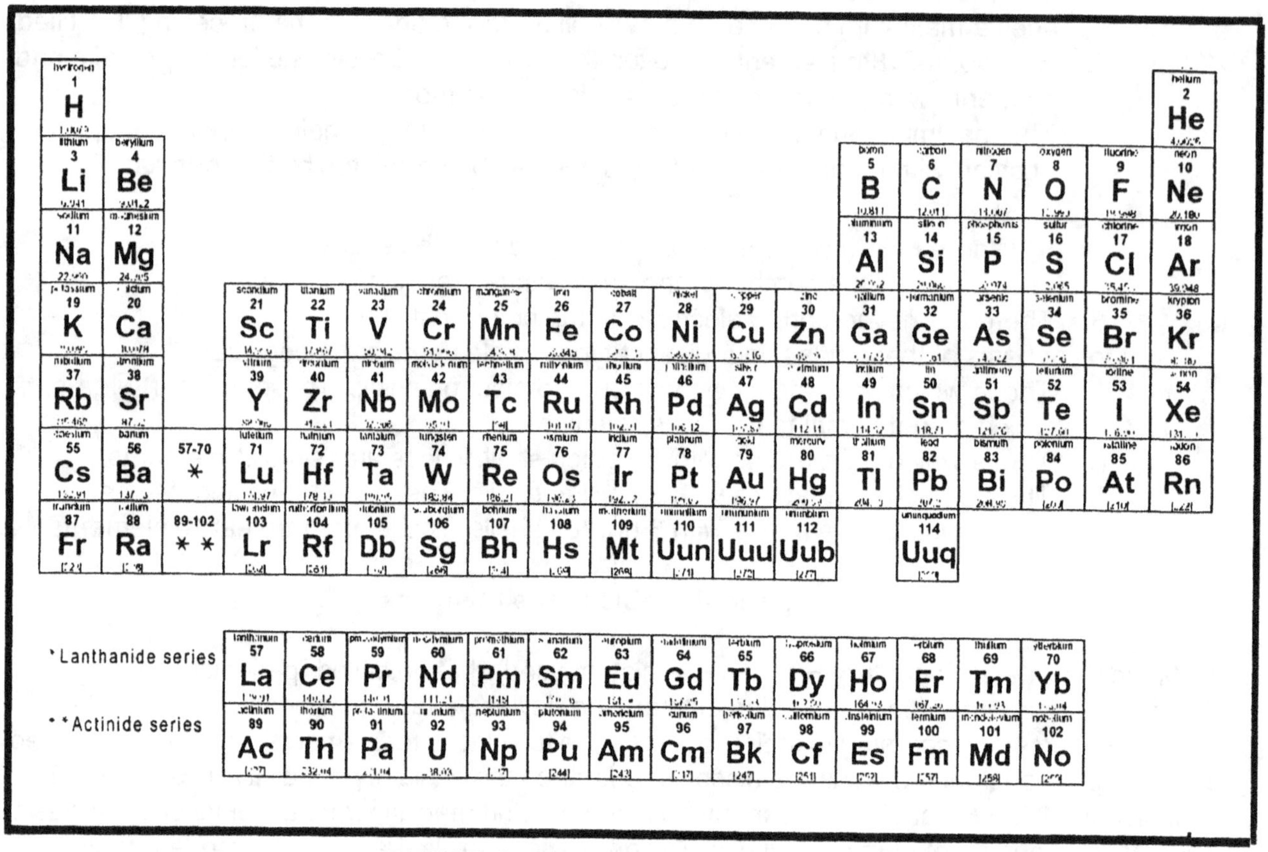

[Periodic Table of Elements]

PERIODIC TABLE OF ELEMENTS

Valence and Atomic Structure

Valence is a term synonymous with "combining power." One may say it is the relative "worth" of an atom of an element in combining with atoms of other elements to form compounds. It is expressed in small whole numbers ranging from 0 to 7 and these numbers may be either positive or negative. Loss of 1 electron from the outermost electron shell confers positive valence of 1 upon an atom; similarly, loss of 2 electrons confers positive valence of 2. Gain of electrons in the outermost shell confers negative valence. Referring to the periodic table (Figure 14), atoms of elements in Groups I, II, and III tend to lose electrons and therefore tend to become positively charged atoms since loss of an electron results in an excess of positively charged protons over negatively charged electrons.

Atoms of elements in Groups IV, V, VI, and VII tend to gain electrons and therefore tend to become negatively charged. It follows that positively charged atoms of Groups I, II, and III attract and are attracted to negatively charged atoms of Groups V through VII resulting in formation of electrically neutral chemical compounds. Sharing of electrons in this manner is known as covalence and is the basis for formation of all chemical compounds.

Unexplained as yet is the question as to why elements of Groups I, II, and III tend to lose electrons and elements of Groups IV through VII tend to gain electrons. The explanation is suggested by the arrangement of the electrons in the outermost shell of these elements. The most stable situation is where the outermost shell has 8 electrons. Group VIII elements are of this type. The tendency for atoms to lose electrons varies in this order: Group I, Group II, Group III, and the tendency for atoms to gain electrons varies in this order: Group VII, Group VI, Group V and Group IV. The strongest tendency toward combination lies, therefore, in those atoms which are furthest from the center of the periodic table. It will be noted on study of the table that this is associated with the number of atoms in the outermost shells. Atoms of Group I elements have a very strong tendency to lose electrons to atoms of Group VII elements because loss of the lone electron in the outermost shell of a Group I atom gives it a more stable configuration and gain of a single electron by an atom of a Group VII element completes its full complement of eight and thus gives it a more stable configuration.

There are other more complex aspects of valence than those outlined here but these must be left to more complete chemical texts.

Valence and Chemical Combination-Valence Number

The "valence number" of an element is the number of electrons of the element associated with formation of a particular compound. Since this number may be different for different compounds of an element, it follows, that elements may have more than one valence number. This fact frequently is difficult for students to understand. To illustrate the point, let us consider the element iron (Fe). Iron combines with oxygen to form 2 different compounds: FeO, a black colored oxide and Fe_2O_3, a red colored oxide. Red iron oxide (rust) is familiar to everyone, black oxide of iron is frequently observed in water plants particularly underneath the scale of cor-roded pipe. Iron also forms numerous compounds with other elements in which it may have a valence number 2 or a valence number 3. Many other elements also have more than one valence number depending upon the chemical compounds involved. Since no one can remember all of the facts, such as these, regarding the various elements and compounds, chemists make frequent use of reference works which present these facts in tabular form.

Laws of Chemistry

Over many years of observation some relationships in the field of chemistry seem to prevail without deviation and, because of this, these have become known as "laws." It is appropriate at this time that some of these be set down so that the reader may be aware of them.

"The Law of Conservation of Matter" was one of the first to be recognized by early chemists. It may be stated in various ways. One of the simplest is "Matter can neither be created nor destroyed in a chemical reaction; it can only be changed from one form to another."

"The Law of Definite Proportions" states that "when a given compound is formed by the combination of elements the proportions, by weight, of the element making up the compound are always the same regardless of the mode of formation of the compound." Thus the proportion, by weight, of hydrogen to oxygen in the compound water (H_2O) is always the same regardless of the source of the water or the manner of its formation.

"The Law of Multiple Proportions"–If 2 or more compounds are composed of the same elements, the different weights of one element which combine with a fixed weight of another stand to each other in the ratio of small whole numbers. We can illustrate this by the compounds water (H_2O) and hydrogen peroxide (H_2O_2). Two atoms of hydrogen are found in both compounds but the number of atoms of oxygen and therefore the weight of oxygen found in hydrogen peroxide is exactly twice the amount found in water. The weight ratio is expressed:

$$\frac{\text{Wt. of oxygen in } H_2O}{\text{Wt. of oxygen in } H_2O_2} = 1/2$$

"The Law of Combining Weight"–In every compound the proportions by weight of each element may be expressed by a definite number (atomic weight) or an integral multiple of that number. This law is essentially an extension of the law of multiple proportions wherein the basic weight of an element (i.e., atomic weight) is included in the statement.

All chemists make use of the principles of chemical measurement through these laws. They enable them to determine the amounts of various elements and compounds required to react with definite amounts of other elements and compounds. It enables them, in short, to make practical use of the science of chemistry.

Molecules, Molecular Weight

Earlier we defined an atom as the smallest part of an element which can exist and retain all of the chemical properties associated with that element. We can now define another unit, "the molecule" as the smallest unit of a compound. Molecular weight of the compound, it follows, is the sum of the atomic weights of the atoms composing the compound.

Equations

A chemical equation is an expression made up of chemical formulae to indicate chemical changes (reactions) which take place when these substances are brought together. For example, we can illustrate what happens when calcium carbonate ($CaCO_3$) is brought into contact with sulfuric acid (H_2SO_4) by writing an equation, $CaCO_3 + H_2SO_4 \rightarrow CaSO_4 + H_2CO_3$. This equation tells us that a reaction takes place and the products of the reaction are calcium sulfate and carbonic acid.

Similarly we can write an equation to illustrate the rusting of iron, $Fe + O_2 \rightarrow Fe_2O_3$. Iron and oyxgen combine to produce iron oxide (rust). In this case the equation as written violates the law of conservation of matter which states that matter cannot be created or destroyed. The violation in this case is the increase of 1 atom of iron on the left side of the equation to 2 atoms on the right side and the increase of 2 atoms of oxygen on the left side to 3 atoms on the right side. We could avoid this by writing the equation $2Fe + 3O \rightarrow Fe_2O_3$, but this is not correct either because gaseous oxygen exists as O_2 not O. To make the equation conform to the facts, we should write it as follows: $4Fe + 3O_2 \rightarrow 2Fe_2O_3$. This process is known as "balancing" an equation. Balancing of simple equations is easily accomplished by inspection. Balancing of complex equations involving a number of reactants and products may be quite difficult. A most important prerequisite for balancing any equation is that the identity of all of the reactants and products be known and their formulas be recorded correctly.

Chemical Calculations

Chemists make practical use of equations to calculate the amounts of reactants required to produce desired amounts of products, to determine the amount of one reactant required to match a. given amount of another reactant, and for similar purposes. To illustrate the method, let us consider again the equation for rusting of iron by oxygen:

$$4Fe + 3O_2 \rightarrow 2Fe_2O_3$$

From Table I, we determine the atomic weight of iron is 55.85 and the atomic weight of oxygen is 16. Then 4 atoms of iron (Fe) are equivalent to 4 X 55.85 = 230.40. A molecule of oxygen contains 2 atoms of O (2 X 16.0) and 3 molecules of oxygen are equivalent to 3 X 2 X 16.0 = 96.0. A molecule of iron oxide is equivalent to 2 X 55.85 (the weight of 2 atoms of iron) plus 3 X 16.0 (the weight of 3 atoms of oxygen), a total of 111:70 + 48.0 = 159.70. Two such molecules of iron oxide then equals 2 X 159.70=319.40. The calculation corresponding to the equation is therefore:

$$4Fe + 3O_2 \rightarrow 2Fe_2O_3$$

4 X 55.85 + 3 X 16.0 X 2 = 2 X 55.85 X 2 + 3 X 16.0
223.40 + 96.0 = 319.40

Thus we know the 223.40 parts by weight of iron react with 96.0 parts by weight of oxygen to yield 319.40 parts by weight of iron oxide. Weight units may be anything, grams, pounds or tons, etc., but, of course, the unit chosen must be used consistently for all of the reactants and products of the reaction.

Equations and calculations of this kind are of great value to all who work with chemical processes including water plant operators. Suppose, for example, a water plant operator wishes to know the amount of alkalinity present in the water he is treating. The alkalinity of the water has influence on the coagulation process and it is desirable that its measure be known so that the amount of coagulants added may be sufficient but not excessive. Alkalinity is measured by reacting those chemicals in the water which are associated with alkalinity with a standard solution of sulfuric acid, that is, a solution of sulfuric acid in water made up to a definite concentration. The standard solution used for this purpose is one which has 0.9806 gram of H_2SO_4 in every 1,000 ml of the solution, that is 0.9806 mg of acid per ml of solution. Using a process called titration, (to be explained later), the exact amount of acid solution required to react with the alkalinity in 100 ml of the water sample, is determined. Let us suppose that it is 25.0 ml. We can now calculate the amount of calcium carbonate (alkalinity) in the water sample using as a basis the reaction between sulfuric acid and calcium carbonate. Thus:

$$CaCO_3 + H_2SO_4 \rightarrow CaSO_4 + H_2CO_3$$

Referring to Table III where the atomic weights of all of the elements involved in this equation are given we find:

$$CaCO_3 = \underset{40.08}{Ca} + \underset{12.01}{C} + \underset{3 \times 16.00}{O_3} = 100.9$$

$$H_2SO_4 = \underset{2 \times 1.01}{H_2} + \underset{32.06}{S} + \underset{4 \times 16.00}{O_4} = 98.06$$

$$CaSO_4 = \underset{40.08}{Ca} + \underset{32.04}{S} + \underset{4 \times 16.00}{O_4} = 136.03$$

$$H_2CO_3 = \underset{2 \times 1.01}{H_2} + \underset{12.01}{C} + \underset{3 \times 16.00}{O_3} = 62.03$$

writing these values under the equation, we get

$$CaCO_3 + H_2SO_4 \rightarrow CaSO_4 + H_2CO_3$$

$$100.9 + 98.06 \rightarrow 136.12 + 62.03$$

Now 25 ml of standard H_2SO_4 solution contains 25.0 X 0.9806 mg of H_2SO_4 and 100 ml of water contains X mg of $CaCO_3$ and the following proportion expresses the relationship between these amounts

$$\frac{X}{100.09\,mg} = \frac{25 \times 0.9806\,mg}{98.06\,mg}$$ when the equation is solved we find that X= 25.01 mg in the 100 ml of sample.

If we wish to express this in terms of mg of $CaCO_3$ alkalinity per liter of sample (the usual practice) we multiply the result by ten (since one liter is ten times 100 ml.)

Thus, $\frac{25\,mg}{100\,ml} \times 10 = 250\,mg/liter$, alkalinity.

Equations commonly used in water plants for purposes of calculation are:

$Cl_2 + H_2O \rightarrow HCl + HOCl$
$Ca(OCl)_2 + Na_2CO_3 \rightarrow 2NaOCl + CaCO_3$
$Al_2(SO_4)_3 + 3CaCO_3 + 3H_2O \rightarrow Al_2(OH)_6 + 3CaSO_4 + 3CO_2$
$CO_2 + H_2O \rightarrow H_2CO_3$
$CaCO_3 + H_2CO_3 \rightarrow Ca(HCO_3)_2$
$Ca(HCO_3)_2 + Ca(OH)_2 \rightarrow 2CaCO_3 + 2H_2O$
$Ca(HCO_3)_2 + Na_2CO_3 \rightarrow CaCO_3 + 2NaHCO_3$
$NH_3 + HOCl \rightarrow NH_2Cl + H_2O$
$NH_2Cl + HOCl \rightarrow NHCl_2 + H_2O$
$NHCl_2 + HOCl \rightarrow NCl_3 + H_2O$
$CaCO_3 + H_2SO_4 \rightarrow CaSO_4 + H_2CO_3$
$Ca(HCO_3)_2 + H_2SO_4 \rightarrow CaSO_4 + 2H_2CO_3$

Ionization

Many elements combine with each other spontaneously on contact. This combination may take place slowly or rapidly and in some instances even explosively. Combinations of elements to form compounds are influenced by many factors such as heat, moisture, or catalytic agents-agents which promote a reaction but do not themselves undergo any change during the reaction. Most chemical reaction takes place in the presence of water because water has a property of splitting some molecules dissolved in it into positively and negatively charge atoms which are called "ions." The process of producing ions is called "ionization" and a molecule which produces ions when dissolved in water is said to "ionize" or "dissociate into ions." Ionization is illustrated graphically as an equation, thus

$NaCl \rightarrow Na^+ + Cl^-$

The charged atoms are called ions.

Positively charged ions are designated "cations" and negatively charged ions are designated "anions." The charges must be equal in magnitude and opposite in sign, otherwise the solution itself would have a charge and this is not the case.

When a molecule dissociates in water, the charges must be such that they equalize even when there are more atoms of one kind than another in the molecule. Example, ferric chloride ($FeCl_3$) ionizes as follows:

$FeCl_3 \rightarrow Fe^{+++} + 3Cl^-$

15

Radicals

Some molecules dissociate or ionize to yield groups of atoms, positively charged cations or negatively charged anions. Ammonium chloride (NH_4Cl) ionizes, $NH_4Cl \rightarrow (NH_4)^+ + Cl^-$ where $(NH_4)+$ is ammonium cation and $Cl-$ is chloride anion. Another example, sodium sulfate (Na_2SO_4) ionizes, $Na_2SO_4 \rightarrow 2Na^+ + (SO_4)^{--}$. In this instance there are two sodium cations and one sulfate anion. Combinations of atoms acting as a unit, such as $(NH_4)+$ and $(SO_4)^{--}$ are called "radicals."

Equilibrium

In writing equations to illustrate a reaction an arrow is often used to indicate the course of the reaction. Sometimes, however, 2 arrows ($\rightleftarrows$) or an equal sign (=) are used and this practice is probably more correct because not all reactions progress to the point where there is complete disappearance of the reactants. In most cases there is a state of equilibrium where reactants and products are present simultaneously. This state of equilibrium is best illustrated in an equation as a double arrow ($\rightleftarrows$). An equilibrium state may be shifted in one direction or another by physical and chemical factors such as heat, acidity, alkalinity or physical removal of one of the products. Chemical manufacturing processes are designed to take advantage of such factors to increase the yield of a desired product and to suppress the yield of an undesired product. Chemical equilibrium is attained also in ionization. Not all substances which dissolve in water ionize, however, and many ionize only to a very slight degree. In the following paragraphs we will discuss various types of substances in relation to ionization.

Acids, Bases, and Salts

An "acid" is a substance which yields $H+$ ions when it dissociates in water. Some examples:

HCl (hydrochloric acid) ($\rightleftarrows$) $H^+ + Cl^-$. This is an acid which ionizes almost completely and for that reason it is considered a very strong acid. Referring: to an acid as "strong" is another way of saying it yields a high concentration of hydrogen ions.

H_2S (hydrogen sulfide) ($\rightleftarrows$) $2H^+ + S^{--}$. This is a very weak acid because its degree of ionization is very low.

Hydrochloric (HCl), nitric (HNO_3) and sulfuric (H_2SO_4) are among the strongest acids and carbonic (H_2CO_3), boric (H_3BO_4) and hydrosulfuric, another name for hydrogen sulfide (H_2S) are among the weakest acids. There are many others which are intermediate between these extremes.

A "base" is a substance which yields hydroxyl $(OH)^-$ ions when it dissociates in water.

A base which yields a high concentration of hydroxyl ions is a "strong" base and one which yields a low concentration of hydroxyl ions is a "weak" base.

Examples: $NaOH \rightleftarrows Na^+ + (OH)^-$ a strong base

$Ca(OH)_2 \rightleftarrows Ca^{++} + 2(OH)^-$ a weak base

$Fe(OH)_3 \rightleftarrows Fe^{+++} + 3(OH)^-$ a weak base

"Salts" ordinarily yield neither hydrogen nor hydroxyl ions. Sodium chloride dissociates as follows: $NaCl \rightleftarrows Na^+ + Cl^-$. Since neither H^+ or OH^- ions are produced, NaCl is a neutral salt neither acid or alkaline. Other salts which are products of a reaction between a strong acid and a weak base, such as aluminum sulfate $Al_2(SO_4)_3$ are acidic because when they ionize a secondary reaction takes place as follows:

$Al_2(SO_4)_3 \rightarrow 2Al^{+++} + 3(SO_4)^{--}$

$H_2O \rightleftarrows H^- + (OH)^-$

$2Al^{+++} + 3H + OH^- \rightleftarrows Al(OH)_3 + 3H^+$

$Al(OH)_3$ is not ionized as much as water itself and therefore aluminum ions remove hydroxyl ions from water to form an undissolved solid thus leaving an excess of H^+ ions in solution. There is no tendency for H^+ ions to combine with $(SO_4)^{--}$ because H_2SO_4 almost completely dissociates. The phenomenon illustrated above where a salt reacts with water, is called "hydrolysis." A similar but converse situation prevails with salts formed from a weak acid and a strong base. Sodium carbonate is an alkaline salt because of ionization, carbonate ions $(CO_3)^{--}$ tend to remove H^+ ions from solution by forming very slightly ionized carbonic acid and thus leaving an excess of $(OH)^-$ ions present in the solution.

A few salts such as mercuric chloride ($HgCl_2$) do not ionize appreciably even though they are slightly soluble in water. They are exceptions to the general rule, however.

pH Value

As mentioned previously, water ionizes to a slight degree producing both hydrogen and hydroxyl ions:

$H_2O \rightleftarrows H^+ + (OH)^-$

It may be said that water is both an acid and a base because it produces both hydrogen and hydroxyl ions. Since these are present in identical concentrations, however, water is considered neutral. It is known that water ionizes to the extent that the concentration of each of the ions, H^+ and $(OH)^-$, is $\frac{1 \text{ molecular weight}}{10,000,000}$ per liter.

A short mathematical way of writing this concentration is $\frac{1}{10^7}$ M (molecular weights per liter) or, still shorter, 1×10^{-7}M (molar, a term discussed later in this chapter). This is a very small number and chemists, like most people, prefer to use numbers which are easier to comprehend. The term "pH" was suggested to designate hydrogen, ion concentration and the term was defined as "the logarithm of the reciprocal of the hydrogen ion concentration."

Thus hydrogen ion concentration = $\frac{1}{10^7}$ Molar, the reciprocal of the hydrogen ion concentration = 1×10^7 and the logarithm of the reciprocal of the hydrogen ion concentration (pH)=7.0. Since, as we noted previously, in pure water the hydrogen ion concentration equals the hydroxyl ion concentration $_p(OH)$ also equals 7.0. From a chemical law, called "The Law of Mass Action", we know that whenever water is present $H^+ \times (OH)^- $ = a constant value = 1×10^{-14}, or, in other words pH+p(OH) =14.

It is not necessary, therefore, for us to determine both pH and p(OH); all we need to do if p(OH) is desired is measure pH (with an instrument designed for the purpose) and subtract the value from 14. There are several water treatment processes, notably chlorination and coagulation, which are affected by pH of the water. These will be discussed in later chapters of this manual.

The pH scale. Table II lists the hydrogen ion concentrations in terms of molecular weight in grams per liter of solution versus the corresponding pH.

Table II

A gram molecular weight Of H+ ions per liter (M)	B reciprocal of A	C Log B (pH)
1.0	1.0	0
0.1	10	1
0.01	100	2
0.001	1,000	3
0.0001	10,000	4
0.00001	100,000	5
0.000001	1,000,000	6
0.0000001	10,000,000	7 (neutrality)
0.00000001	100,000,000	8
0.000000001	1,000,000,000	9
0.0000000001	10,000,000,000	10
0.00000000001	100,000,000,000	11
0.000000000001	1,000,000,000,000	12
0.0000000000001	10,000,000,000,000	13
0.00000000000001	100,000,000,000,000	14

(Acid: pH 0–7; Alkaline: pH 7–14)

Careful examination of this table discloses several important facts
1. When the hydrogen ion concentration is highest, pH is lowest.
2. When the hydrogen ion concentration is lowest, pH is highest.
3. Neutrality at pH 7 is midpoint in the scale; pH values lower than 7 represent higher hydrogen ion concentration (more acid) than neutrality and pH values higher than 7 represent lower hydrogen ion concentrations (more alka-line) than neutrality.
4. pH values between the values listed in column C represent hydrogen concentration lying between those listed in column A and column B. For example, pH 5.5 represents a H⁻ ion concentration of 0.00000316 gram molecular weight/liter (3.16×10^{-6} gram molecular weight/liter). The value 0.00000316 would appear in column A and the corresponding value in column B is 316,000.

Equivalents of Acids and Bases

An equivalent weight of an acid is the weight of an acid which will supply one gram molecular weight of H+ ions (1.0 gram) in a liter of a solution of the acid in water. For acids which ionize to produce one H^+ ion per molecule of the acid, an equivalent weight of the acid is the same as its molecular weight. These are called "monoacids." These acids which produce 2H+ ions per molecule of the acid (example, $H_2SO_4 \rightarrow 2H^+ + (SO_4)^{--}$) are called "diacids" and those acids which produce $3H^+$ ions per molecule example $H_3PO_4 \rightarrow 3H^+ + (PO_4)^{---}$) are called "triacids."

It follows that an equivalent weight of a monoacid is equal to the molecular weight of the acid in grams, an equivalent weight of a diacid is equal to 1/2 of the molecular weight of the acid in grams and an equivalent weight of a triacid is equal to 1/3 of the molecular weight of the acid in grams.

A similar situation exists with respect to bases. A "monobase" produces an equivalent weight of hydroxyl ions (17 grams) when one molecular weight of it is present in water solution; a dibase produces an equivalent weight of hydroxyl ions when 1/2 of the molecular weight of the substance is present in one liter of water solution and a tribase produces an equivalent weight of hydroxyl ions when 1/3 of the molecular weight of the substance is present in one liter of water solution.

The term "equivalent" is not restricted to acids and bases. A further discussion of its significance will be found under *Solutions*.

Neutralization of Acids and Bases

Consider what happens when an acid solution and an alkaline solution each containing one equivalent of hydrogen ions and hydroxyl ions respectively, are mixed:

$HCl \rightleftarrows H^+ + Cl^-$ acid

$NaOH \rightleftarrows Na^+ + (OH)^-$ base

The H^+ ions and the $(OH)^-$ ions combine to form water which is only slightly ionized. The effect is to remove $H+$ and $(OH)^-$ from the system until they are almost all gone. When the reaction is completed the only H^+ and $(OH)^-$ ions left are the insignificant concentration obtained from ionization of water. There are, of course, free Na^+ and Cl^- ions present in abundance because NaCl is a highly ionizable salt. This type of reaction involving acids and bases is called "neutralization" and is very common in chemistry.

Indicators Titration

An indicator is a substance which changes color according to conditions which prevail in a reaction system. In the mutual neutralization of HCl and NaOH described above, an indicator of the proper type would indicate by a sharp color change the instant neutrality is attained. If one solution is added in increments of small volume to the other solution containing the indicator a sharp color change at the attainment of neutrality enables the chemist to exactly match the two solutions. This process is called "titration" and a more detailed discussion of it will follow later in this chapter. The indicators used for acid-base titrations are sensitive to pH and a very slight shift of pH at the point of neutrality brings about a striking change in color of the solution even though the amount of indicator added is usually very small. There are many indicators used in chemistry and some of them are sensitive to reactions other than pH change. Among these are oxidation-reduction indicators and indicators which form colored compounds on chemical combination with a reactant or a product of a reaction.

Solutions

Since most chemical reactions take place while the reactants are in solution, it is important that facts pertaining to solutions and their properties be well understood.

A solution is made up of 2 or more components. One component is the "solvent" which dissolves the other component or components, each of which is called a "solute." Both the solvent and the solute may be in various physical states, that is solid, liquid, or gaseous. For example, we may have a solution of a solid in a liquid, a gas in a liquid, a solid in a solid, and other combinations. It is also possible to have a combination of more than one solute in a single solvent.

Some solutes are infinitely soluble in a solvent; ethyl alcohol, for example, is soluble in water in all proportions. These two substances may be said to be mutually soluble. Most solutes have only limited solubility in a solvent, however, and when the solubility limit is reached no more will be dissolved. The solvent and the excess solute exist then in two distinct phases which may be liquid-liquid, liquid-solid or liquid-gaseous.

Concentration of Solutions. There are a number of terms used with reference to concentration of solutions which must be understood.

A *concentrated solution* is one where the amount of solute in a given volume of solvent is relatively great.

A *dilute solution* is one where the amount of solute in a given volume of solvent is relatively small.

Obviously these two terms are not definite with respect to amount.

Percentage Concentration. More precise terminology is available for expressing the concentration of a solute in a solvent. "Percent concentration" is often expressed as the

$$\frac{\text{weight of the solute}}{\text{weight of the solvent}} \times 100.$$

This is a more accurate way of expressing concentration than the terms "concentrated" or "dilute" but it too is unsatis-factory from a practical standpoint because it is difficult to weigh large volumes of liquids. Frequently percent concentration is considered to mean

$$\frac{\text{weight of the solute in gram}}{100 \text{ ml of solvent}}$$

This implies that 100 ml of any solvent weighs 100 grams- an unjustified assumption if accurate measure is desired. It is, however, a reasonably close approximation if water is the solvent.

Still another interpretation of "percent concentration" is possible

$$\frac{\text{weight of solution}}{\text{weight of solution}} \times 100.$$

This is the most accurate of the 3 definitions for percentage concentration but again it could become necessary to weigh large volumes of solution.

Molar Concentration., Because of the different definitions possible for "per cent concentrations" chemists have adopted the term "molar concentration" which means 1 mole of solute per liter of solution. A mole is 1 formula weight of solute in grams. Thus sodium chloride (NaCl) has the formula weight

Na + Cl = NaCl
22.99 g + 35.45 g = 58.54 g

A mole of sodium chloride, therefore, weighs 58.54 grams and a 1 molar solution of sodium chloride equals 58.54 g of sodium chloride per liter of solution *(not per liter of solvent)*. This is a very precise way of expressing concentration and suitable for most routine work. For the highest possible accuracy, however, the temperature of the solvent must be taken into account since liquids expand and contract as the temperature rises or falls. When making "standard" solutions a chemist adjusts the temperature to the level at which the solution will be used to avoid changes in concentration. Molar concentration is abbreviated "M"; thus a 1 molar solution is written 1 M.

Normal solution. Another way of expressing concentrations of solutions is in terms of normality. A "normal" solution is defined as a solution containing 1 "equivalent" per liter. The term "equivalent" was used before in discussion of acids and bases. For acids, one equivalent was described as the weight of an acid which would supply one gram molecular weight of H^+ ions (1.0008 grams) in a liter of solution of the acid in water. For bases, it was described as the weight of a base which would produce one gram molecular weight of $(OH)^-$ ions (17.008 grams) in a liter of a solution of the base in water. Such concentrations of acid and bases can also be called "normal" solutions for a "normal" solution is described as one which has 1 equivalent weight of the substance per liter of solution and by the same token all normal solutions are equivalent to each other. Normal concentration is abbreviated "N"; thus a 1 normal solution is written 1 N. In the discussion of acids and bases the term "equivalent" was introduced to explain the meaning of "mono", "di", and "tri" acids and bases. In the foregoing discussion of normality the term equivalent was also used to explain the meaning of normality.

It is important to understand that "equivalency" and "normality" do not refer to acids and bases alone or to ions alone but refer to salts as well as acids, unionized elements as well as ions and to compounds as well as elements. Both normality and equivalency are related to atomic weight and valence. Thus: equivalent weight of an element =

$$\frac{\text{atomic weight of the element}}{\text{valence of the element}}$$

Examples:

Equivalent weight of sodium (Na) = $\frac{22.997}{1}$ = 22.997

Equivalent weight of calcium (Ca) = $\frac{40.08}{2}$ = 20.04

In the use of this expression it is important, to note that valence of an element is not always the same. Copper (Cu) has an equivalent weight of 63.57 in the "cuprous" state where the valence is 1, but in the "cupric" state where its valence is 2, it has an equivalent weight of 31.785.

$$\text{Equivalent weight of a compound} = \frac{\text{molecular weight of the compound}}{\text{total positive valence of compound}}$$

Examples:

Equivalent weight of barium chloride ($BaCl_2$) =

$$\frac{137.36 + 2 \times 35.457}{2} = \frac{137.36 + 70.914}{2} = 104.137$$

Equivalent weight of filter alum $Al_2(SO_4)_3 \cdot 12H_2O$ =

$$\frac{2 \times 26.97 + 3(32.06 + 4 \times 16) + 12(2 \times 1.008 + 16)}{3(\text{valence of Al}) \times 2(\text{no. of Al atoms})} =$$

$$\frac{53.94 + 3(32.06 + 64) + 12(2.016 + 32)}{6} =$$

$$\frac{53.94 + 3 \times 96.06 + 12 \times 18.016}{6} =$$

$$\frac{53.94 + 288.18 + 216.192}{6} = \frac{558.312}{6} = 93.052$$

Equivalent weight of cupric chloride ($CuCl_2$) =

$$\frac{63.57 + 2 \times 35.457}{2} = \frac{63.57 + 70.914}{2} = \frac{134.484}{2} = 67.242$$

Equivalent weight of cuprous chloride (CuCl) = $\frac{63.570 + 35.457}{1}$ = 99.027

Standard solutions. a standard solution is a solution which is made so accurately that it can be used to determine the concentration of substances in other solutions provided there is reaction between them which proceeds to a definite endpoint detectible by an indicator for example a standard solution of an acid can be used to determine the concentration of a base and the base solution is then said to be "standardized against" the acid. The base solution can then be used to standardize other acids. In this manner concentrations of many solutions are measured and all of the measurements can be referred to the original standard acid which is called the "primary" standard.

Primary standards - To be useful as a primary standard a substance must meet certain requirements which insure its stability under all usual environmental conditions.
1. it must be chemically pure
2. it must be a solid at ordinary temperatures
3. it must not readily absorb water from the air
4. it must not decompose at ordinary drying temperatures of 100-110° C

The United States Bureau of Standards have available a number of chemical compounds which meet these requirements and they can be purchased directly from the Bureau. Laboratory supply houses also supply primary standard chemicals for various purposes. These are listed in reagent catalogs issued by the individual firms.

Titration–a technique known as tritration is used to match an unknown reagent to a standard reageant. In addition to the two solutions, an appropriate indicator to detect the enpoint of the reaction between them, a beaker, a stirring rod, a burette, and a support for the burette are required. A burette is a glass tube open at the top and fitted with a stopcock on the lower end. The tube is graduated to measure accurately the volume (in milliliters) of the standard solution placed in it. The beaker contains an accurately measured volume of the solution to be assayed. One or two drops of the indicator are added to the beaker and while the liquid in the beaker is continuously stirred the standard solution is added in small increments. As the reaction progresses with each addition the amount of excess reagent in the beaker becomes smaller and its eventual exhaustion will be apparent by a sharp color change of the indicator: there is a direct relationship between the volume of standard solution used and the volume and concentration of the unknown solution in the beaker. For titrations involving normality this relationship is expressed:

volume of standard X normality of standard =
volume of unknown X normality of unknown
Transposing terms, we find normality of unknown =

$$\frac{\text{volume of standard} \times \text{normality of standard}}{\text{volume of unknown}}$$

The technique of titration is used extensively in water chemistry. Determinations of chloride, hardness, alkalinity, oxygen consumed value, chemical oxygen demand and biochemical oxygen demand all depend upon a titration procedure in the analytical method. More detailed information on this subject is given in the chapter "Laboratory Procedures."

Organic Chemistry

This is a specific branch of chemistry concerned with compounds of carbon. Carbon is unique among all other elements not only because its reactivity is great but also because of its ability to combine with itself in various ways to form a very large number of compounds. Many of the compounds of carbon were first isolated from living i.e. "organic" materials. It soon became apparent that all plant and animal tissue is composed of numerous carbon atoms in combination chiefly with hydrogen and oxygen but also to a much lesser degree with nitrogen, phosphorous, sulfur and metals.

Carbon has a valence of 4 and it is usually represented graphically as $-\underset{|}{\overset{|}{C}}-$.

The valence bonds shown must be shared with other atoms or groups of atoms for a stable structure. This can be done in various ways.

Examples:

```
    H  H  H  H
    |  |  |  |
H - C- C- C- C - H
    |  |  |  |
    H  H  H  H
       Butane
```

Carbon atoms in a straight chain. Here the 10 valence bonds are shared with hydrogen atoms to form the hydrocarbon butane- a well known combustible gas.

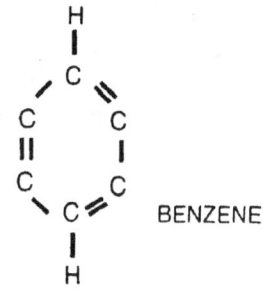

3-Methyl Pentane

Carbon atoms in a branched chain forming the hydrocarbon 3 methyl pentane.

The $H-\underset{|}{\overset{|}{C}}-H$ group is called methyl and

it is attached to the third carbon in a 5 membered chain.

Carbon atoms in a ring formation with 6 reactive valence bonds. This is known as the "benzene" ring because if the available reactive sites are occupied by hydrogen atoms, the resulting compound is benzene. Thus:

BENZENE

These are but two representatives of many thousands of carbon compounds in existance. The possibilities for new combinations are almost endless and new organic compounds are constantly being made synthetically. Many of the natural organic substances, for example, chlorophyll the green coloring matter in plants are extremely complex materials, and organic chemists may spend years first determining their structure and many more years learning how to sythesize them from simpler compounds.

Some of the organic materials to be found in water have defied the best efforts of chemists to identify them. Recently developed instruments such as gas-liquid chromatographs, infra-red analyzers and mass spectrometers are important tools aiding the chemists in this work. Identification and measurement of the concentration of the many kinds of pollutants which enter our water courses is an essential part of water pollution control. With increasing population density and increased industrialization of our country the variety and quantity of materials natural and synthetic, organic and inorganic, which enter our water courses threatens the usefulness of these streams for drinking water sources, recreational use and even industrial purposes. The role of chemistry in preservation of our greatest natural resource, water, is all important.

Table III

Chemicals Associated with Water Quality and Water Treatment

Chemical Name	Common Name	Chemical Formula
Ammonia	Ammonia	NH_3 (Ammonia gas) NH_4OH (Ammonia solution)
Alminum sulfate	Filter alum	$Al_2(SO_4)_3 \cdot 14H_2O$
Calcium carbonate	Limestone	$CaCO_3$
Calcium bicarbonate	....	$Ca(HCO_3)_2$
Calcium hydroxide	Hydrated lime or slaked lime	$Ca(OH)_2$
Calcium oxide	Unslaked lime or quick lime	CaO
Chlorine	....	Cl_2
Chlorine dioxide	....	ClO_2
Copper sulfate	Blue vitriol	$CuSO_4 \cdot 5H_2O$
Ferric chloride	....	$FeCl_3 \cdot 6H_2O$
Hydrochloric acid	Muriatic acid	HCl
Sufuric acid	Oil of vitriol	H_2SO_4
Sodium chloride	Salt	$NaCl$
Sodium carbonate	Soda ash	Na_2CO_3
Sodium bicarbonate	Soda	$NaHCO_3$
Sodium hydroxide	Lye	$NaOH$
Sodium phosphate	....	$Na_3PO_4 \cdot 12H_2O$
Fluosilicic acid (hydrofluosilicic acid)	....	N_2SiF_6
Sodium fluosilicate	....	Na_2SiF_6
Sodium fluoride	....	NaF
Carbon	Activated carbon	C

www.ingramcontent.com/pod-product-compliance
Lightning Source LLC
Chambersburg PA
CBHW080321020526
44117CB00035B/2590